Jossey-Bass Guides to
Online Teaching and Learning

Making Online Teaching Accessible

INCLUSIVE COURSE DESIGN FOR STUDENTS WITH DISABILITIES

Norman Coombs

JOSSEY-BASS
A Wiley Imprint
www.josseybass.com

Published by Jossey-Bass

A Wiley Imprint

989 Market Street, San Francisco, CA 94103-1741—www.josseybass.com

Readers should be aware that Internet Web sites offered as citations and/or sources for further information may have changed or disappeared between the time this was written and when it is read.

Limit of Liability/Disclaimer of Warranty: While the publisher and author have used their best efforts in preparing this book, they make no representations or warranties with respect to the accuracy or completeness of the contents of this book and specifically disclaim any implied warranties of merchantability or fitness for a particular purpose. No warranty may be created or extended by sales representatives or written sales materials. The advice and strategies contained herein may not be suitable for your situation. You should consult with a professional where appropriate. Neither the publisher nor author shall be liable for any loss of profit or any other commercial damages, including but not limited to special, incidental, consequential, or other damages.

Jossey-Bass books and products are available through most bookstores. To contact Jossey-Bass directly call our Customer Care Department within the U.S. at 800-956-7739, outside the U.S. at 317-572-3986, or fax 317-572-4002.

Jossey-Bass also publishes its books in a variety of electronic formats. Some content that appears in print may not be available in electronic books.

Library of Congress Cataloging-in-Publication Data

Coombs, Norman, 1932-
  Making online teaching accessible : inclusive course design for students with disabilities / Norman Coombs.
      p. cm. – (Jossey-bass guides to online teaching and learning ; 17)
    Includes bibliographical references and index.
  ISBN 978-0-470-49904-7 (pbk.)
  1. Students with disabilities–Computer-assisted instruction.   2. Computers and people with disabilities.   3. Inclusive education.   I. Title.
  LC4024.C66 2010
  371.9'04334–dc22

                                                                          2010026647

FIRST EDITION

PB Printing   10 9 8 7 6 5 4 3 2

CONTENTS

LIST OF FIGURES

PREFACE

The explosion of online learning is one of the results of recent developments in information technology. Another is that, with the access provided by assistive applications, people with disabilities now have an exciting world of previously unavailable information at their fingertips. This specialized software and (sometimes) hardware, generally referred to as assistive or adaptive technologies, includes software that magnifies the onscreen image, reads aloud text from the computer or Internet, recognizes spoken commands and dictation, or provides an onscreen alternative to a physical keyboard.

People who were formerly labeled "print disabled" can now transcend that designation because today's digitized content is display-independent: it can be presented in multiple modes, in whatever way works best for the particular user. As a result, online learning has the potential to provide a learning space that is fully accessible to the formerly print disabled without compromising its quality.

In my opinion, a major reason that more progress hasn't been made toward providing better access to online learning for students with disabilities is because explanations of how to achieve this goal almost immediately become bogged down in arcane technical details. Administrators fear that the process will be unduly expensive. And faculty fear that providing for these students will mean that they have to become information technology experts.

This book endeavors to address these fears and shortcomings in part by showing that instead of having to understand the behind-the-scenes technology, everyday content-authoring applications that faculty are already familiar with—such as Microsoft Word—will do that for them. This means creating online content that is accessible to students with disabilities is much easier—and probably far less expensive—than people fear. The goal of this book is to demystify the processes and technology involved—to make them accessible to those of us who are "tech-impaired"—and to demonstrate both the benefits and necessity of learning these new skills.

WHAT DOES "ACCESSIBILITY" MEAN?

In the context of this book, the word *accessibility* means that online course content can be effectively used by people who fall into the following disability groups:

- Students who are blind, or who have severe visual impairments but are not legally blind
- Students with upper body motor impairments (those with other types of motor impairments should not have difficulties in an online context)
- Students with either visual or cognitive processing difficulties (commonly called learning disabilities)
- Students with hearing impairments

FOR WHOM IS THIS BOOK INTENDED?

This book is primarily intended for teachers and instructional design staff involved in creating course content. However, others will also find some or all of the chapters relevant, including information technology staff responsible for maintaining the learning management system (LMS) and the institution's main Web site, student disability services staff, and administrators from all departments that are directly or indirectly involved in online learning.

Faculty and instructional design staff are already focused on taking subject matter content and adapting it for delivery online. Although some may have the technical expertise to learn and follow all the established standards and guidelines for making Web content accessible to students with disabilities, most have neither the interest nor the time it would require. For these readers, the book will demonstrate how they can continue to use the authoring tools they already know and, by following a few tips and better practices, output content that will achieve functional accessibility.

Information technology staff have the background to understand the technical details of accessibility set forth in the Web Content Accessibility Guidelines by the Web Accessibility Initiative and the Section 508 standards established by the government. This book, however, will enable you to see the problems from the more human viewpoint of faculty and students.

Staff from departments for students with disabilities will have a background in understanding how various disabilities affect the learning experiences of different students and will have familiarity with the assistive technologies these students use. This book will familiarize you with the accessibility barriers and their solutions involved in online learning. In turn, this familiarity will enable you to bring your skills and knowledge to support both the faculty and the students.

Administrators will come to understand the importance of making online learning accessible for students with disabilities. The last chapter sets forth some ideas for administrators to empower online faculty and staff to enable students with disabilities to succeed in their online courses.

WHAT WILL YOU FIND IN THIS BOOK?

Chapters One and Two provide a high-level look at accessibility issues related to online learning: how people with disabilities use computers, an overview of universal design principles, a brief discussion of relevant legislation and internationally agreed-upon guidelines, the problems and benefits of online learning for students with disabilities, the accessibility of commercial learning management systems, and general recommendations for how best to ensure online content is accessible.

Chapters Three through Seven provide concrete tips on how to create online content that will fully include students with disabilities. Chapters Three through Five focus on using Microsoft Word, Excel, and PowerPoint in ways that enhance the accessibility of online content. Chapter Six specifically deals with the particular issue related to providing access to math and graphics content. Chapter Seven focuses on the accessibility of multimedia presentations and how to use alternative modes of communication to ensure and enhance access to course content.

Chapter Eight deals with the broad issue of how to provide support for accessible online learning at the institutional level. This chapter focuses less on faculty concerns and more on staff and administration responsibilities.

WHY DOES ACCESSIBILITY MATTER?

As a society, we have decided that providing access to public buildings and transportation for people who are unable to walk is the right thing to do, and have incorporated that decision into building codes and other laws. Similarly, closed captioning is provided for most television programming and movies on DVD. Other examples are legion, but equal access to education has, for a host of reasons, lagged behind. That gap is rapidly being closed, thanks in no small part to advances in technology.

Because you have picked up this book, it is likely that you already have some interest in offering online learning experiences that will be more accessible for students with disabilities, but you may not yet have much understanding of how your investment of time and effort can pay off for others down the line. If so, perhaps the following story will illustrate.

I lost my sight in a play accident when I was eight years old and relied on Braille and tape recordings for my formal education from then on. In spite of having to use these cumbersome tools, I earned a Ph.D., taught history for twenty-five years, and published a book, *Black Experience in America*.

Finally, though, I caught a break. In the mid-1980s, a colleague nagged me to try the Apple computer in the psychology lab that was connected to a voice synthesizer. I resisted, wondering what a historian would do with a computer. Shortly after trying it, however, I found I was able to both write class handouts and proofread them. I discovered e-mail, and began to communicate with colleagues and friends on campus and across the country—and I didn't have to find someone to read my messages to me: the computer and synthesizer did it instead.

But my real awakening came when I realized that if students sent me their *papers* in e-mail, I could read them by myself, at any time of the day or night. I wouldn't have to set up an appointment with a reader to read them to me. Suddenly I had far more freedom and independence. I also made another discovery:

One of my students started a running e-mail exchange with me about the details of the paper she had sent and my grading. After a few messages back and forth she told me that, because she was deaf, this was the first time she had "talked" with a teacher without relying on an intermediary!

A short time later, when the college was searching for a teacher to experiment with adding computer communication to enrich a telecourse, I realized that although I'd thought I had no interest in distance learning, I already had that experience—I had been using computer communications as a teaching tool. The distance learning department never imagined that their one volunteer would be a historian and not a technology person, and they certainly never imagined the volunteer would be blind. This is the only time in my life that blindness was an advantage. For me, the computer was already a communication tool, whereas others still saw it as just a computational device.

In 1987, I delivered a presentation at a conference on distance education at the Open University at Milton Keynes, England. In 1990, New York State honored me with the Teacher of the Year Award for this distance education work.

Besides helping to pioneer the distance learning program at the Rochester Institute of Technology, I have taught online for the New York School for Social Research, San Diego State University, the University of Southern Maine, and the University of Washington. Since retiring in 1997, I have been the CEO of EASI: Equal Access to Software and Information (http://easi.cc). EASI provides a number of online courses to inform faculty and staff about accessible information technology, and also provides regular Webinars so that busy faculty and staff can participate live while working at their desks.

Several years after I began traveling and presenting on accessible learning, the colleague who had originally pressured me to try a computer told me that I had changed: I was more poised and self-confident, he said.

I believe that creating accessible online learning experiences for students with disabilities can do even more than give them a quality education—it can empower them to become stronger, more self-reliant people.

ACKNOWLEDGMENTS

This book is dedicated in memory of my close friends and working colleagues, Richard Banks and George Buys, who were instrumental in introducing a history professor to the world of accessible information technology. I still miss their friendship and support. I also owe a debt of gratitude to Erin Null, Associate Editor at Jossey-Bass, for encouraging me to tackle this book as a way to move beyond this loss. I also want to thank Alison Knowles and Cathy Mallon, Jossey-Bass editors, for their patient attention to the process of preparing the document for publication.

Elizabeth Coombs served faithfully through the entire process as my research assistant, for tracking down references, for capturing the screen shots, and for continuously reminding me of the importance of details. Marisol Miranda provided me with invaluable information about technology details with which I was not familiar.

The clarity and flow of the book content was guided by the tireless work and patience of my main editor, Leslie Tilley. Thank you, Leslie, for improving my book.

I also thank my wife, Jean, for encouraging me when I became discouraged and ran low on enthusiasm.

ABOUT THE AUTHOR

Norman Coombs earned his Ph.D. in history from the University of Wisconsin in 1961 and taught history at the Rochester Institute of Technology for almost forty years. Currently, Coombs is the CEO of EASI (Equal Access to Software and Information, http://easi.cc). EASI uses Webinar and online courses to assist universities, schools, and businesses in making their information technology accessible to people with disabilities. Coombs' goal is to take the jargon out of accessible information technology enabling nontechnical faculty to create course content that removes barriers to learning for students with disabilities.

Coombs was awarded a Fulbright scholarship to study in England in 1959 and was awarded a National Endowment for the Humanities grant in 1969. He was the key investigator for three National Science Foundation grants to disseminate information on accessible information technology. In 1990, he was nominated as the Council for Advancement and Support of Education (CASE) Teacher of the Year in New York state for his work in distance learning. He has received several other national awards for his work in advocating for the accessibility of online learning for students with disabilities. (Coombs himself has been blind since he was eight years old.) He has presented on the topic at conferences in the U.S., Canada, Mexico, and half a dozen European countries.

His publications include *Black Experience in America* (1972) and *Information Access and Adaptive Technology,* coauthored with Carmela Cunningham in 1997.

He and his wife Jean now live in Laguna Hills, California. They have two daughters and two grandchildren. He can be contacted at norm.coombs@gmail.com.

Making Online Teaching Accessible

Creating a Level Learning Space

The emergence of information technology has changed the education process for everyone, and it has transformed most people's personal lives as well. This truth is even more important for people with what, for the purposes of this book, I will call print and audio disabilities. Those with print disabilities need special help to surmount the obstacle posed by books and other printed materials. Lectures and other audio content present a similar barrier for those with hearing impairments.

Digitized information has been a major breakthrough for these people. Because it is display independent, it can be rendered in different modes for various purposes. In the past, traditional textbooks froze information in a single format: it was stored as print and a human intermediary or translator was needed to output it into any other form. Digitized information, however, is stored as numbers and this allows it to be printed out, displayed on a computer monitor, or even projected onto a screen so that it can be seen from the rear of a lecture hall. Specialized assistive software can render the same information in even more formats, thus providing students who have disabilities with timely and effective access to the information and creating the potential for a more level learning space for all.

This chapter has three main topics: assistive technologies, universal design, and laws and guidelines relevant to online instruction. People with disabilities often use special software—generally called assistive technology or adaptive technology—in conjunction with computers. These technologies assist the user and at the same time adapt the computer's input and output systems to accommodate a wider spectrum of people's needs. The universal design movement takes a different approach. Instead of focusing on making accommodations for people with special needs, it urges designers to create devices and content to include the broadest segment of the population possible. Finally, the chapter gives an overview of the laws and official guidelines in effect mandating that products and content be created in ways that will not discriminate against people with special learning needs or unique working styles or both.

HOW PEOPLE WITH DISABILITIES USE COMPUTERS

As a provider of online course content, you may not really need to know how people access your content. It may not matter, for example, whether an individual is using a smart phone, a laptop computer, or a desktop computer in a college computer lab. But if you found out that a significant proportion of your students were accessing your lessons from a phone, you might design some content differently based on that knowledge.

Similarly, although it's not absolutely essential that you know about the assistive computer software used by students with various disabilities, that awareness can help you design your online content in ways that won't create needless barriers to their learning. And the good news is that you can employ universal design features while still using the standard content authoring tools you already use. Let's look at the assistive technologies most commonly used by students in accessing online course content. These technologies are available for a variety of computer platforms: Mac, Windows, and Unix-based operating systems. You'll also "meet" some typical users to get an idea of how some of your students are experiencing your course material.

Voice Recognition Technology

Voice recognition software allows the user to control the computer by speaking commands aloud and to dictate to input text into documents. Users of this type of technology are those who cannot—or cannot easily—use a standard keyboard because of motor function, visual, or certain types of learning disabilities. People with dyslexia, for example, can use a keyboard, but because they frequently jumble the sequence of letters both in reading and writing, dictating permits them to bypass this hurdle.

Penny, an auto mechanic, was in her twenties when an accident left her a quadriplegic. Thanks in part to voice recognition software, she now holds a staff position in a Pennsylvania community college, where, among other tasks, she trains faculty on how to better serve students with disabilities.

On-Screen Keyboards

People with motor impairments that prevent them from using a standard keyboard frequently use an onscreen equivalent. The computer cursor moves across an image of a keyboard at the bottom of the monitor. When it reaches the desired letter or symbol, the user triggers a single switch to input that letter into the computer. For people with little or no use of their hands and arms, the computer can track the user's eye movement so no muscle movement is required to trigger the switch. To speed this process, the onscreen keyboard can be combined with software that predicts the desired word based on the first few letters.

As a daring teenager, Grant dove off a cliff into too-shallow water. His neck was broken, but Grant did not let that end his active life. He used an on-screen keyboard to attend college in California, earn his bachelor's degree, and move on to productive employment.

Screen Magnification Software

Although most software applications permit the user to enlarge the screen interface and content on the monitor, the amount of enlargement allowed is limited, and often the image is degraded. Commercial screen magnification software, however, will maintain the integrity of the image while permitting enlargement from two to sixteen times normal. Obviously, this benefits people with visual impairments. Advanced screen magnification software also has the ability to use a synthetic voice to speak text, although this capability is not robust enough to meet the needs of someone who has very little or no sight.

Screen magnification software combined with speech output can also benefit people with visual and cognitive processing disabilities. Although they don't need the larger image, a by-product of enlargement is that less information appears on the screen at one time. For some students with learning and cognitive disabilities, a computer display packed with information can be overwhelming, so simplifying it increases their ability to read and learn the content. The software will also highlight the word being spoken by the synthesized voice. This provides dual sensory input for the user, reinforcing learning and helping the user to focus on the content.

At a university in Wisconsin, Dick was a student whose poor sight required him to wear strong glasses to read. But as his sight further degraded, the glasses no longer worked well enough. With the aid of screen magnification software Dick was able to do his assignments through the computer, which enabled him to finish his college degree.

Dick had a work study job training students with disabilities on assistive technology. Lora, one of his students, had dyslexia and struggled to keep up with all the reading required for her courses. Screen magnification helped her to better decode the text and understand the lessons. Having the text that was being spoken highlighted made it easier for her to concentrate.

Screen Readers

Screen reading software uses synthetic speech to tell the user (usually someone who is blind) what is on the monitor and to confirm that the key is being pressed when writing. This enables the student to both write and proofread class assignments. Universities are now providing books in electronic format, which is accessible to this software, thus enabling the student to work independently whenever it is convenient.

Screen reader software essentially looks at the document displayed on the computer monitor, hunting for anything that is coded as text. In simple terms, when it locates text, it uses a complex logarithm to come up with the sounds for each letter. Next it looks for any further language rules that modify what sound it should make. For example, it has rules telling how to pronounce the letters "ough" in different ways for the words *bough, cough, dough, rough,* and others.

John was a successful science professor at a major university when, due to a rare condition, he lost vision in both eyes in a very short time. Instead of surrendering his dreams and hopes, he learned about the assistive technologies that could enable him to continue functioning as a professional. The computer was already a basic tool he used in his work, and he quickly became a proficient screen reader user. Not only did he continue university teaching, but John also became the principal investigator on several grants from the National Science Foundation.

Audio Transcriptions and Video Captioning

Transcriptions of audio content such as subtitles and closed captioning for video existed long before these media became digitized. The change to digital media has made creating both audio and video easier and less expensive. A production team and studio are no longer required, so captions are becoming more common while the need is increasing. Recorded audio of class lectures is common, and it is necessary to have transcriptions available for any students who cannot hear that recording. Captioning and audio transcriptions are required by various pieces of legislation that mandate equal education for students with disabilities. A video, even if it is of high quality and very informative, is almost useless for anyone who is deaf and therefore misses all of the verbal content. The same is true of an audio recording. It has no value for someone who is deaf. When there are captions and transcriptions, these students can acquire the information and can learn the content as do other students.

After losing her hearing as a young adult, Mary attended the National Technical Institute for the Deaf at the Rochester Institute of Technology. Because her ability to read American Sign Language was still poor, Mary struggled to follow class lectures. However, she registered for an online course that used captioned videos and an asynchronous, online text discussion. Mary says that the mix of captioned videos and a text discussion for class participation made this her most meaningful college course.

When information is digitized, people with the difficulties like those described above are able to access information independently. Although people with such disabilities have long succeeded in schools and universities without the benefit of these leveling tools, they also had to spend time and energy overcoming cumbersome hurdles to obtain their education. Many have gone on to succeed in professional careers while still facing these barriers every day. Now their world is opening with fresh opportunities and exciting new independence.

UNIVERSAL DESIGN AND ONLINE LEARNING

On October 28, 2009, the U.S. Government Accountability Office submitted a report to the Committee on Education and Labor of the House of Representatives entitled "Higher Education and Disability: Education Needs a Coordinated Approach to Improve Its Assistance to Schools in Supporting Students" (U.S. GAO report GAO-10–3, 2009). The report noted that schools are increasingly using the universal design model in curriculum development and delivery. In this context, online learning is one of the many delivery platforms benefiting from the inclusion of universal design.

What Is Universal Design?

Universal design is the design of products and environments to be usable by all people, to the greatest extent possible, without the need for adaptation or specialized design.

—Ronald Mace (Center for Universal Design, 2008)

Mace earned a degree in architecture from North Carolina State University in 1966, where, as a wheelchair user, he encountered many barriers. He believed that instead of modifying specific facilities to meet the needs of certain users, all facilities should be designed to accommodate as broad a population as possible (Center for Universal Design, 2008). The goal of universal design when applied to education is to make learning inclusive for all students, not just those with disabilities. It is an approach to designing all products and services to be usable by students with the widest possible range of both functional (physical) capabilities and different learning styles.

Seven Principles of Universal Design

The following general principles were developed by the Center for Universal Design and have become widely recognized as a summary of the vision of the universal design movement. The list below is based on version 1.0 of the principles, dated April 1997. The Center's Web site has a wealth of universal design resources and can be found at www.design.ncsu.edu/cud.

1. *Equitable use*—The design should be appealing, useful, and marketable to people with diverse abilities rather than being targeted at a specific segment of the population.

2. *Flexibility in use*—The design accommodates a wide range of individual preferences and abilities. It should accommodate right- and left-handed people and let the user work at his or her own pace.

3. *Simple and intuitive*—Use of the design is easy to understand, regardless of the user's experience, knowledge, language skills, or current concentration level. It should also provide effective prompting and feedback during and after task completion.

4. *Perceptible information*—The design should communicate necessary information effectively to the user, regardless of ambient conditions or the user's sensory abilities. One way to do this is to use different modes (pictorial, verbal, tactile) for redundant presentation of essential information and provide adequate contrast between essential information and its surroundings.

5. *Tolerance for error*—The design should minimize the adverse consequences of accidental or unintended actions. The design should provide warnings of possible errors and provide fail-safe features.

6. *Low physical effort*—The design should allow the user to use the item efficiently and comfortably with a minimum of fatigue.

7. *Size and space for approach and use*—The design should allow everyone access and use of all components regardless of body size, posture, or degree of mobility. It should also accommodate assistive devices or personal assistance.

I will look at how these principles apply to designing online content shortly. In later chapters that deal with content creation, I show how, with little effort or learning, you can use these universal design principles to make your course content inclusive.

Universal Design for Learning

The seven principles of universal design are generic and were originally conceived in the context of physical architecture. The question of how to apply them to education is outlined by the movement known as Universal Design for Learning (UDL; National Center on Universal Design for Learning, 2010). The movement was developed at the Center for Applied Special Technology (CAST), a nonprofit research and development organization founded in 1984. This initiative deals with general education issues and, as a result, its principles can be more readily applied to the classroom than to online learning. However, its experience in working toward universal design in classroom education is a good foundation on which to develop concepts relevant for online learning.

CAST describes UDL as a flexible approach to curriculum design that offers all learners full and equal opportunities to learn. Based on research into the diverse ways people learn, UDL offers practical steps for giving everyone the chance to succeed. CAST believes that some people are visual learners, some learn by doing, and some by hearing and has developed a set of guidelines that can include all these learners.

Online learning, by its basic nature, limits the availability of some of the learning modalities discussed by CAST. For example, a math problem can only be solved online by manipulating numbers on the computer, not by manipulating physical objects, as can be done in a live elementary school classroom. As a result some of the CAST universal design for learning principles may have limited applicability for online learning. Nevertheless, the concept of looking for ways to accommodate the unique skills of online learners is worth considering.

Based on recent research in neuroscience, CAST has identified three primary brain networks and has used these to establish three primary principles that guide its UDL guidelines.

Provide Multiple Means of Representation Because students have different learning styles and needs, it is important to ensure that key information is equally perceptible to all students by

- Providing the same information through different sensory modalities (e.g., through vision, hearing, or touch)
- Providing information in a format that will allow for adjustments by the user (e.g., text that can be enlarged, sounds that can be amplified)

Information should be displayed in a flexible format so that the following perceptual features can be varied:

- The size of text or images
- The amplitude of speech or sound
- The contrast between background and text or image
- The color used for information or emphasis
- The speed or timing of video, animation, sound, simulations, and so forth
- The layout of visual or other elements

This principle applies as much to online as to classroom learning.

Provide Multiple Means of Action and Expression Students differ in the ways that they can navigate a learning environment and express what they know. For example, individuals with significant motor disabilities may have problems navigating electronic text on a computer or in handling a book. They may also have trouble using a pen or using the computer keyboard. Both learning and cognitive disabilities may cause problems related to reading and writing.

In reality, there is no one means of expression that will be optimal for all. The item that will be most relevant for designing online content is ensuring that there is a keyboard alternative for any mouse action so that students can use common assistive technologies that depend on those commands.

Provide Multiple Means of Engagement   Teachers devote considerable time and effort to designing content that will grab their students' attention and engagement. But students differ significantly in this respect—what engages one person will bore another. Therefore, it is important to incorporate alternative means of attracting and maintaining interest. One of the most successful ways to get any student's attention is to give him or her choices and opportunities for personal control. Offering students choices can develop self-determination and pride in accomplishment and increase the degree to which students feel connected to their learning. Online delivery provides a rich array of ways to add interest and attractiveness to content, including graphics, audio, video, and more. However, as I discuss later, be sure that such items are not just distractions that draw students' focus away from the main topic of the presentation (Center for Applied Special Technology, 2010).

LEGISLATION, DECISIONS, AND GUIDELINES GOVERNING ONLINE LEARNING

Legislation and guidelines on any subject are usually designed to be broad and generic. Instead of having specifics related to online learning, they will set forth general principles related to education or access to information technology. In this discussion I briefly describe relevant laws and guidelines and point to how they relate to online learning.

From the faculty perspective, the concerns are both how to fulfill them and how much doing so will influence teaching. In most cases, these requirements will affect how content is delivered much more than the content itself. Although there is a mandate to make courses accessible to students with disabilities, a legal exemption exists for situations in which an adaptation would fundamentally alter the nature of the program. For example, making a music appreciation course accessible to someone who is totally deaf would make fundamental changes to the course. However, this exemption very seldom applies.

Relevant U.S. Federal Legislation

In the United States, two pieces of federal legislation contain statements about education and students with disabilities that have come to bear on college and university online learning: the Rehabilitation Act, both Sections 504 and 508, and the

Americans with Disabilities Act, Title II. In the following section I briefly describe the parts that have been interpreted as having relevance for online learning. In a later section I discuss those same portions of the laws in the context of cases that have come before the Department of Education's Office for Civil Rights (OCR).

Section 504 of the 1973 Rehabilitation Act   In 1973, the Web and online learning as we know them had yet to come about, so the Rehabilitation Act contains no language specifically addressing online learning. Section 504 has been amended a couple of times in the intervening years, but it still is framed in broad terms. Nevertheless, it is regularly cited by OCR as bearing on its decisions.

The Web site of the Department of Justice (DOJ) says that "The Rehabilitation Act prohibits discrimination on the basis of disability in programs conducted by Federal agencies, in programs receiving Federal financial assistance, in Federal employment, and in the employment practices of Federal contractors." In referring more specifically to Section 504, the page further says that "no qualified individual with a disability in the United States shall be excluded from, denied the benefits of, or be subjected to discrimination under" a program or activity that receives federal financial assistance (U.S. Dept. of Justice, 2005).

The relevance of this legislation for online learning is that any educational program must be made accessible to students with disabilities. Because this is an institutional requirement, you should remind the school of its obligation at budget time.

Section 508 of the 1973 Rehabilitation Act   Section 508 was amended in 1998 to specifically cover electronic information and the information technologies used to display it. The legislation plus training resources and constantly updated information are available on the Web (http://section508.gov). Section 508 is primarily a federal procurement law: it mandates the federal government to purchase only information technologies and equipment that meet its requirements and to produce only information that meets these standards. The standards cover the operability of equipment and the accessibility of information, including Web pages.

Section 508 has already produced four results:

- More government information on and off the Web is becoming available in accessible formats.

- Because the government comprises such a large market, vendors are beginning to pay more attention to accessibility issues.

- Several state governments have adopted Section 508 or similar standards for their state, and these standards are affecting educational institutions.

- Although Section 508 may not technically apply to education, courts are relying on its standards to assist them in measuring Web accessibility. As a result, these standards are finding their way into legal practice.

Title II of the Americans with Disabilities Act The Americans with Disabilities Act, Title II (28 CFR PART 35), says that the act "prohibits discrimination on the basis of disability in employment, State and local government, public accommodations, commercial facilities, transportation, and telecommunications" (Americans with Disabilities Act, 1990). Frequently cited by the Department of Education's Office for Civil Rights in its investigations, Title II requires that state and local governments give people with disabilities "an equal opportunity to benefit from all of their programs, services, and activities (e.g., public education, employment, transportation, recreation, health care, social services, courts, voting, and town meetings)." Title II does provide some qualifications. The act says that "Public entities are not required to take actions that would result in undue financial and administrative burdens." They are required to make reasonable modifications to policies, practices, and procedures, except when doing so would "fundamentally alter the nature of the service, program, or activity being provided."

DECISIONS OF THE DEPARTMENT OF EDUCATION'S OFFICE FOR CIVIL RIGHTS

OCR is the entity legally responsible for receiving and investigating complaints of discrimination against colleges and universities.

In every official response to a complaint, OCR asserts its legal authority by citing Title II and Section 504 of the Rehabilitation Act of 1973, including the regulations implementing these acts, specifically 34 Code of Federal Regulations, Part 104, which prohibits recipients of federal financial assistance from discriminating on the basis of disability in programs and activities (see, for example, U.S. Dept. of Education OCR, 1997). When OCR investigates a complaint, its function is not to assign guilt and administer punishment. Its goal is to guarantee that the student receives the rights enshrined in Section 504 and in Title II, and it wants to help the college in fulfilling these responsibilities. The implied threat—the withdrawal of federal funds—has never happened because all parties prefer to work for a resolution. Although an OCR visit may be something between embarrassing and unpleasant, the office can also bring its expertise to help the college with its responsibilities, thereby making the visit a benefit.

Each of OCR's decisions is based on a specific complaint, so much of the documentation is specific to that narrow instance.

Effective Communication

In a 1997 letter to California State University, Los Angeles, OCR said that Title II of the Americans with Disabilities Act requires that "communications with persons with disabilities [must be] as effective as communications with others." This covers "any transfer of information including … the verbal presentation of a lecturer, the printed text of a book, and the resources of the Internet" (U.S. Dept. of Education Office for Civil Rights, 1997). In the previous year, in a letter to San Jose State University, OCR noted the rapidly growing importance of the "information superhighway" and the importance of computer technology in fostering independence for students with disabilities. However, OCR also noted that graphic images commonly used on the Web are not accessible for people using screen reader software (U.S. Dept. of Education Office for Civil Rights, 1996).

These OCR letters do not yet refer to online learning, which was still in its infancy. However, this awareness of the importance of providing effective communication on the Web can readily be translated to an online learning environment.

The meaning of this decision for online learning is that accessibility issues can result in communication that is not equally effective for all students. To avoid being in violation of this provision, online content providers need to design for accessibility.

Timeliness of Delivery

In 2003, OCR responded to a complaint it had received against California State University, Fullerton. The letter said,

In construing the conditions under which communication is "as effective as" that provided to non-disabled persons, on several occasions OCR has regarded the three basic components of effectiveness as *timeliness of delivery* [emphasis added], accuracy of the translation, provision [of the content] in a manner and medium appropriate to the significance of the message and the abilities of the individual with the disability." (U.S. Dept. of Education Office for Civil Rights, 2003)

In responding to other complaints, OCR again insisted that a service including a communication must be timely. (In terms of providing alternative versions of print material, it previously recognized that the length of the print document made a difference in what would be reasonable to consider as timely.) In the resolution, CSU Fullerton agreed to "provide alternate media to students with disabilities at the same time educational materials are provided to non-disabled students in the same class." This includes course texts. The resolution set forth dates for faculty to select books and for students to register for the class so that the college would know what book was required for what course and by which student (U.S. Dept. of Education OCR, 2003).

The first way this impacts online learning is that when a print text is required, the college is obliged to obtain an alternative version for students with disabilities. Undoubtedly, the college will already have a system in place to handle this for its on-campus students. This system should also be available to meet the needs of online students as well.

Second, accessible versions of online course content must be provided in a timely manner as well. This means posting content in an accessible format rather than retrofitting it later. One place where this may be relevant is in providing transcriptions for audio and captions for video. The other place it may be relevant is if in some course, accessibility required making and delivering hard-copy Braille or tactile graphics for a student with a disability. These materials should be created and sent to the student ready for use when that online lesson is due.

Undue Burden

In the 1997 letter to CSU Los Angeles mentioned previously, OCR set the bar for qualifying for an "undue burden" exemption so high as to be almost unattainable. OCR stated that "When a public institution selects software programs and/or hardware equipment that are not adaptable for access by persons with disabilities, the subsequent substantial expense of providing access is not generally regarded as an undue burden when such cost could have been significantly reduced by considering the issue of accessibility at the time of the initial selection."

This can be compared to the process of creating sidewalk ramps for people who use a wheelchair. If that access was not included in the original design, the curb would have to be broken up and replaced with a new cement ramp—at some cost. But forming the ramp when a sidewalk is poured requires little extra work and is thus much cheaper. The same is true for other design projects: it's more efficient and less costly to build in access than to add it later.

REVIEW OF OCR DECISIONS AND ONLINE LEARNING

To sum up, the key concepts that OCR uses in its decisions that relate most directly to information technology and online learning are these:

- Communication for people with disabilities must be as effective as that provided to others
- Effective communication for people with disabilities must be delivered in a timely manner

Obviously, online learning is communication and consequently is covered by these concepts.

International Web Accessibility Laws and Standards

The International World Wide Web Consortium (W3C) formulates standards for Web design. One of the W3C's initiatives is the Web Accessibility Initiative (WAI), which has set forth technical guidelines to make Web pages accessible to people with disabilities and to the adaptive technologies they commonly use. As of this writing, the WAI Web site lists the policies or legislation or both of the following political entities dealing with Web accessibility: Australia, Canada, Denmark, European Union, Finland, France, Germany, Hong Kong, India, Ireland, Israel, Italy, Japan, New Zealand, Portugal, Spain, Switzerland, the United Kingdom, and the United States. It also list similar policies of Canada's provinces and those of individual states in Australia and the United States (see www.w3.org/WAI/Policy).

Web Content Accessibility Guidelines

In late 2008, WAI issued version 2 of the Web Content Accessibility Guidelines (WCAG 2.0). While the guidelines are highly technical and complex and fill more pages than this book, WAI summarizes them as follows (W3C, 2008; emphasis in original):

Perceivable

- Provide **text alternatives** for nontext content.
- Provide **captions and alternatives** for audio and video content.
- Make content **adaptable**; and make it **available** to assistive technologies.
- Use **sufficient contrast** to make things easy to see and hear.

Operable

- Make all functionality **keyboard accessible**.
- Give users **enough time** to read and use content.
- Do not use content that causes **seizures**.
- Help users **navigate and find** content.

Understandable

- Make text readable and understandable.
- Make content appear and operate in predictable ways.
- Help users avoid and correct mistakes.

Robust

- Maximize **compatibility** with current and future technologies.

Let's look at how these four principles relate to both the universal design and universal design for learning principles described earlier in this chapter:

- *Perceivable*—The fourth of the seven universal design principles states that information should be perceptible, and all three of the UDL principles deal with both perception and comprehension.

- *Operable*—The second of the seven principles urges that design include flexibility in use to accommodate a wide range of individual preferences and abilities. Likewise, the second UDL principle states that learning design should provide "multiple means of action and expression." In this context, "operable" refers to the design of a Web page permitting users to interact with it in several different modes to suit their individual needs.

- *Understandable*—The first WCAG principle is limited to perception, which is not the same as comprehension. This principle deals with the ability of users with different learning styles and needs to understand the content. Both the universal design principles and the UDL principles combine perceivable and understandable into a single criteria.

- *Robust*—This WCAG principle does not have an equivalent in the universal design or UDL principles, but it's not a bad idea. You would definitely want your online materials to be compatible with current Web standards and able to function for as long as necessary.

The Web Content Accessibility Guidelines are not legal mandates, but they are internationally recognized as technical standards and they influence legislation in many countries. In the United States, the Section 508 Web standards *are* requirements and they are similar to many of the basic principles of WCAG.

TAKE-AWAYS FROM THIS CHAPTER

Because digitized information is display independent, schools and universities now have the opportunity to create a learning space that puts students with disabilities on a more level playing field than ever before. This is particularly true for online learning, which is entirely digital. Whether this potential is realized depends in part on whether the systems are based on principles of universal design and conform with information technology standards and with relevant legislation.

Online learning specifically is made or broken by the institution's Web infrastructure, including the learning management system it selects, and faculty and staff normally have little input into such decisions and selections. However, an awareness of the issues discussed in this chapter will help faculty and staff provide intelligent input when and as they can.

An instructor's responsibility is primarily to author course content that will facilitate access for students with disabilities, rather than causing needless barriers.

The legislation cited in this chapter makes it clear that providing accessible content is a legal requirement for the institution, its staff, and its faculty—but providing a quality education to all students should be a more useful motivator than is the threat of the law.

The Department of Education's Office for Civil Rights, instead of trying to punish those who fall short of the target, seeks to assist schools needing help to live up to these responsibilities. This book seeks to show that it is possible to achieve a significant degree of accessibility by continuing to use authoring tools that faculty already know and use.

Online Learning and Students with Disabilities

Chapter One demonstrated the potential information technology has for opening a new and exciting window on the world for people with disabilities. This chapter focuses more directly on the specific advantages and disadvantages of online learning *systems* from these students' point of view.

A report from the American Foundation for the Blind (American Foundation for the Blind, 2008) noted that access to online learning depended on three things:

- The accessibility of the learning management system
- The accessibility of the actual course content
- The skill of the student in using up-to-date assistive technology

In this chapter I examine those three "legs" of the online learning tripod. First, I will look at the accessibility of distance learning programs' Web sites and learning management systems. Second, I look at the accessibility of course content. Finally, I discuss the skills and equipment students need to access online courses via assistive software.

ACCESSIBILITY OF THE ONLINE LEARNING INFRASTRUCTURE

"Online learning infrastructure," as used in this book, means both the learning management system (LMS)—or some custom-built equivalent—and the Web pages that a student must navigate to reach the LMS and the content it houses. It is possible for a system itself to be accessible once you've arrived but for the Web pages that are supposed to provide entry to instead prevent it.

For example, a decade ago, I was invited to an online conference by the vendor who had created the Web conferencing system. They were proud of having included features to make it fully functional for users with disabilities. However, when I went to the URL for the Web conference, I had to agree to a license agreement before being allowed into the virtual room. The Accept button could only be reached with a mouse, and I am unable to use a mouse. I never got into the room to find out whether the vendor's pride in its achievement was merited.

I am not alone in experiencing frustration with some Web and Web-based content. In 2001, Axel Schmetzke conducted extensive research evaluating the accessibility of Web pages of a number of universities, academic libraries, and distance learning organizations (Schmetzke, 2001). Because course content itself is kept behind a password, Schmetzke limited his study to the top level (home page and next layer down) of the Web pages of distance learning programs, 3,366 pages in total. Of the 219 home pages of distance learning programs that Schmetzke checked, he found that only 15.1 percent were free of major accessibility errors. Of the pages directly linked to the 219 home pages, 23.3 percent were free of accessibility errors. The remainder (almost 85 percent and over 76 percent, respectively) were all pages a student with a disability would have to navigate before even accessing the learning management system. Those are sobering figures.

Students' Online Course Experiences

The American Foundation for the Blind (AFB) report mentioned earlier in this chapter was based on a survey of nearly 100 students with disabilities experiences with online courses. The survey was weighted heavily toward students who had limited vision or were blind. The AFB report states that these students found that most features of online educational tools presented significant problems for those using assistive technology such as screen reading or screen magnification software. Nearly one-third of respondents who used assistive technology reported the experiences as being "unreliable," "inconsistent," or "unsuccessful".

The respondents experienced different learning management systems, with about 70 percent having taken courses through Blackboard. Nearly 20 percent of the respondents rated their Blackboard experience as unreliable, inconsistent, or unsuccessful use—which means that some 80 percent did find it to be somewhat useful. However, those using screen magnification (15 percent) found their experience less successful than did those using screen reading software (85 percent). The overall results showed that the average fell somewhere in between the best and worst extremes (American Foundation for the Blind, 2008).

The use of HTML content, when written with proper structure, was the only item that was not mentioned as a problematic feature. Real-time chat features were inaccessible to almost all students, regardless of their assistive software or their disability. PDF files were often reported as problematic for accessibility with screen reading and screen magnification software.

Obviously, this survey used only a small sample, most of whom had limited vision or were blind; other disability groups might report different experiences. Moreover, the students who were evaluating Blackboard could have been using different product versions, and the content authors may have used its features differently, so even students with similar disabilities were not rating identical items. Nevertheless, the survey provides an idea of what students with certain kinds of disabilities experience in trying to access online learning.

The frustration with Learning Management Systems experienced by the students who replied to the AFB survey was supported by the results of a study conducted in 2008 by the California State University Office of the Chancellor (Dennett et al., 2008). The Chancellor's Office had issued an RFP with the goal of finding LMS vendors it could recommend to the 23 CSU campuses. Five LMS products were chosen for evaluation: Desire to Learn, Blackboard, WebCT, Angel, and Moodle. Only the latter two passed the test criteria; the others failed the Section 508 Web standards. Blackboard has subsequently passed those requirements and been added to the list (Kaplan e-mail, 2010).

Issues Common to Most Learning Management Systems

So far, I have talked about infrastructure accessibility issues only in general terms. The issues I describe next are some of those faced by students with disabilities when they enter the learning management system.

Page layout and page navigation are the first accessibility issues to face students when they open a learning management system. LMSs are feature-rich products, and the opening page is usually crowded with text, links, graphics, and much

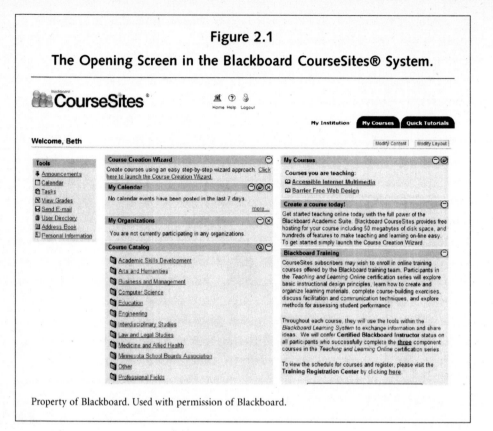

Figure 2.1

The Opening Screen in the Blackboard CourseSites® System.

Property of Blackboard. Used with permission of Blackboard.

more, as shown in Figure 2.1. Although some people may be awed and delighted by all these features, those with learning or cognitive disabilities can be bewildered and intimidated. Someone using screen magnification will see everything at an enlarged scale, so for them only a small portion of the page will be visible.

Many users will be daunted by the complexity of navigating all the frames and dozens of links. Students using an onscreen keyboard or voice recognition or someone who is blind and using screen reader software will have to move from link to link by using the tab key on the keyboard instead of the mouse. Imagine your frustration if the link you want is two dozen or more key presses down the page—and that link might take you to another page where you have almost the identical problem.

One thing you may be able to do to simplify the LMS interface is by identifying features of the system you do not plan on using and have them set to be hidden from the student. Most systems permit the instructor to do this. For example, if you do not plan to use the discussion or the chat, see whether you can hide those links for your course. If you limit the features you use to as few as possible, the LMS page becomes less cluttered. In addition, if there is a way for students to customize the system's display, you can provide instructions on how to do this.

Text Chat

Most LMSs include the ability to conduct real-time text chat. In a classroom discussion, getting students to participate can be a slow and painful process. Text chat, in contrast, is usually rapid fire, with several people texting at the same time. This can sometimes make it difficult to follow the thread of the discussion, and for users with learning or cognitive disabilities the rapid stream of text chat can quickly become overwhelming. Someone with a motor impairment may have little trouble keeping up, but be unable to actively participate, because it takes extra time to respond.

Users of screen readers frequently find text chat inaccessible because of either the chat window's technology or the screen reader's limitations. Because of the different difficulties experienced by students with disabilities, the teacher may want to consider other ways to promote student interaction.

Whiteboard

LMSs frequently include a whiteboard which is normally used in a real-time setting like text chat. Depending on how it is used, it could work well for all the disability groups except for students who are blind. Because the whiteboard is a graphic, screen readers cannot handle the content. Students with learning disabilities frequently learn well with graphic content, and the same is true for students who are deaf. People with upper body motor impairments will have no problem so long as they themselves do not have to work the whiteboard and draw.

CREATING ACCESSIBLE ONLINE COURSE CONTENT

The accessibility of the course content itself is the second requirement for the creation of accessible online learning. The American Foundation for the Blind, in its report discussed earlier in the chapter, noted that some courses actually posed very few of the problems mentioned by students taking the survey (American Foundation for the Blind, 2008). These courses had a number of similarities:

- Consistent designs
- Proper headings
- Fewer frames
- Contrasting colors
- Accessible graphics

As you will see shortly, all of these features align with the principles of universal design discussed in Chapter One. They make the content clearer for people with vision, visual processing, and cognitive disabilities—as well as for those with no obvious impairment. That is, the short list of features that the foundation's survey found that helped students with disabilities are things that are important in creating content that will benefit anyone.

In this section I provide an overview to designing optimally accessible content. The key word here is *overview*—in later chapters I spell out the specific steps you can take to implement these general guidelines. Some ingredients in creating good content design are generic. A few relate specifically to the laws and guidelines discussed in Chapter One.

Be Learner-Centered

Thomas Friedman, in his book *The World Is Flat*, contends that information technology is leveling power relationships (Friedman, 2005). Many online teachers have observed this phenomenon in action and remark how online classroom behavior mirrors the shift of power from teacher to students. This doesn't mean that the students have all the power and the teacher none, but rather that in the online arena the two are now more equal participants—partners even.

Part of the teacher's role in this relationship is to consciously adopt a learner-centered approach to teaching and learning. This pushes us to see the student as someone with unique learning styles and needs, someone who can be helped—or hindered—by the way our online course content is presented.

Modularize and Organize Your Course Content

Dividing lessons into small, "bite-size" pieces—often called "chunking"—has long been advocated as an important learning tool for students with disabilities, especially those with learning cognitive disabilities. Students with hearing impairments whose first language is American Sign Language also benefit from this, as do nonnative speakers without disabilities (Richards, 2008). Ruth Clark (2007) also recommends segmenting online lessons for all learners so that they can be completed in short chunks. Limit asynchronous e-learning lessons to two to five minutes and synchronous e-learning lessons to an hour.

Chunking implies not only that the document is modularized but also that it is well organized. Good structure—or rather, the headings that provide the visible framework—is an aid to content navigation for all users. Using well-thought-out, descriptive headings will enable users with disabilities to navigate quickly through the document, just as do users with normal vision. Skimming a page looking for the next section is a common practice. But for users of some assistive technologies such as screen readers, this is only possible when the document uses properly constructed headers, which enable these users to jump from one header to the next. Otherwise, the user has to read a line at a time to find the next section. (Correct header formatting is a topic I delve into in Chapter Three.)

Provide a Text Equivalent for Every Nontext Element

Section 508, § 1194.22(a) states, "A text equivalent for every nontext element shall be provided (e.g., via "alt", "longdesc", or in element content)." (The 508 standards quoted below are taken from Section 508 Standards, Subpart B—Technical Standards 1194.22 Web-based intranet and Internet information and applications.)

Do not be concerned about the technical jargon. Most refer to HTML Web design. The "alt" does apply to content other than Web pages. A screen reader cannot describe an image, but the author can attach a short, hidden text description to the image which the screen reader will vocalize for its user. (Chapters Three and Four explain how to easily do it.)

We are not advocating text-only course content. Using graphics cannot only make the content more visually appealing and interesting, but also for topics in art or science, for example, they may be essential. A chart or diagram may convey information better than can be done verbally. Some learners, including those with learning disabilities and cognitive disabilities, often learn better from visual representations. That said, it is important not to clutter documents with graphics for the sake of decoration. Ruth Clark (2007) recommends the careful use of *relevant* visuals to promote learning, but strongly advises against adding graphics that do not clearly support the text.

A nontext element can also be an audio lecture. In that case, this provision requires providing a text transcription for people who are deaf.

Include Captions for Multimedia Presentations

Section 508 § 1194.22(b) says, "Equivalent alternatives for any multimedia presentation shall be synchronized with the presentation" (Section 508 of the Rehabilitation Act of 1973). Here "presentation" refers to multimedia such as a video or a narrated PowerPoint slide show that includes a sequence of pictures accompanied by a soundtrack. (The term *transcription* usually refers to text that is not synchronized whereas the term *caption* usually refers to text that is synchronized with a visual presentation.) These provide hearing impaired people with the ability to understand the audio-only content as well as be able to make sense out of a video.

Captions have other uses. A video can be searched via the text in the captions allowing the ability to quickly locate an item without having to sit through the presentation. It also can make a captioned Internet video searchable using an Internet search engine. (Chapter Four, on PowerPoint, discusses transcription of slide show narration, and Chapter Seven, on multimedia, describes at a high level the creation and use of captions and video descriptions.)

Use Color Carefully

§ 1194.22(c): "(c) Web pages shall be designed so that all information conveyed with color is also available without color, for example from context or markup" (Section 508 of the Rehabilitation Act of 1973).

Using color alone to convey meaning can pose a problem for many people, with and without disabilities. Without some kind of key to the colors used, anyone will need to "decode" the information, and this may be particularly difficult for people with some learning disabilities.

Although people with some form of color blindness are not usually considered to have a disability, they will have more difficulty than others when information is encoded by color. The most common form of color blindness is the inability to distinguish between red and green. To illustrate the issue, say that a newspaper article included a map of the United States with the most environmentally conscious states shown in green and the others shown in red.

There is no real problem with using color this way, but there needs to be another way to access the information about the states' environmental leanings, such as a list ranking them from best to worst or an icon in each of the "green" states.

Use Headers to Make Data Tables Accessible

First, let's think about what a table or spreadsheet is and how it works. Tables consist of a matrix of individual cells containing bits of information, like the check register shown below. The entry in a single cell only really has meaning when it is associated with the column and row headers and can be correctly understood in the context of the table as a whole.

NO.	DATE	PAYEE	AMOUNT
124	2/14	Hi Hat Florist	$85.37
125	2/14	Chez Michel	$152.00
126	2/15	Electricon	$93.20
	2/15	Deposit	$2783.21
127	2/18	PlunderMart	$44.97

Because being able to identify the contents of the rows and columns is crucial to understanding a table, both Section 508 § 1194.22(g) and WCAG 2.0 Guideline 1.3.1 specify that row and column headers be used and identified.

One of the strengths of a table is that it presents a lot of isolated information in a compact format, thereby enabling someone to compare data and analyze it thoroughly. However, for someone with either visual processing or cognitive disabilities, the denseness itself can make a table extremely difficult to understand. The reader has to connect the isolated bit of data in a cell to the relevant row and column headers to give it meaning. This visual scanning from cell to header and back can add to the confusion for those with visual and cognitive processing difficulties. For example, someone with dyslexia could have trouble with the relationship between headers and cells.

Students who depend on a screen reader hear the contents of the table read cell by cell. They must then conceptualize the table as a whole—trying to hold all of those individual contents in their mind while painfully compiling a mental picture of the table in its entirety. But this process is made easier if the user knows which row and column contain headers and can use a setting on the screen reader software that speaks the relevant header when it reads a cell's content, thus making its meaning perfectly understandable.

Students who use screen magnification software, rather than a screen reader, have slightly different problems. The screen enlargement software is likely to move parts of the table beyond the edges of the computer's monitor. This becomes a particular problem with bigger tables. The user may be unable to glance up a column or along a row to locate the relevant headers. Instead they will have to use the mouse to scroll up to the top or to the side of the display, thereby losing track of the cell they were trying to understand. Fortunately, the software has some features to assist with this.

As a general guideline, it's best to keep tables on the smaller side. No one, whether they have a disability or not, enjoys reading a huge table onscreen (or, probably, off). Often, overly large tables will be more effective if they are broken up into several smaller ones, including a summary table, if that is appropriate. Also try to provide a summary or explanatory caption just before a table describing what it is about and giving information about its format, especially specifying which row and column contain the headers.

Tables are revisited in Chapter Three, in the context of Microsoft Word and Excel documents.

Web Conferencing

Web conferencing systems sometimes are an integral part of an LMS and sometimes are outside of it somewhere on the Web. These are real-time group events in which people assemble in a virtual learning space. Frequently, a presenter speaks to the group while slides are shown to support the presentation. These systems are both powerful and complex. A lot of background text chatter often occurs between the participants while the speaker is presenting, and, in addition to the difficulty with text chat described above, having several things happening at the same time can present difficulties for those with either learning or cognitive disabilities. In addition, depending on the design of the virtual room, those who rely on using the keyboard to navigate may be overwhelmed by the system's complexity, especially if they are trying to navigate while the presenter is speaking.

This is a clear case of the system's accessibility being dependent on how the instructor uses the system. Web conferencing, more than most other online applications, allows the presenter a number of options in using its features. Which features are used while presenting is as crucial to a Webinar's accessibility as the actual design of the application.

I look at conferencing again in Chapter Seven, on multimedia.

THE STUDENTS' PART OF THE EQUATION

Once you have assured that your content and the delivery system are accessible, as discussed in the preceding sections, the burden is on the student. The third ingredient in creating an accessible online course system is the skill of the student in using up-to-date assistive technology to complete online courses. The following sections briefly outline what you can and should expect from students who have disabilities.

Up-to-Date Technology

Just as someone using a mid-1990s browser will be unable to access most contemporary Web sites, students with disabilities using antiquated adaptive technology will be unable to access many Web features used in their courses. Online learning systems assume that students have computers that, though they may not be the absolute latest, can handle most Web features. It is reasonable to have similar expectations for students with disabilities. Your institution's Web site probably has a page that lists the browsers that work best on the site. That page should also specify which assistive technologies the site was designed to interface with.

Skill in Using Adaptive Technology

It is also reasonable to expect students to know how to use their assistive software, and the more advanced their skill in using it, the quicker they will be able to understand the course content and complete assignments. If a student seems to be struggling with the technology, the staff at your institution who provide student disability services should be able to help them. This office increasingly provides support for the most common assistive technologies, including computers equipped with such applications and offering training on their use.

Departmental lab assistants may also have some limited know-how that can help students with disabilities.

Schools commonly have a help desk to assist students with problems in accessing the schools Web site and other online facilities. The staff is trained to help students troubleshoot common hardware and software problems related to connecting with the university systems. Although it is probably too much to expect them to have advanced understanding of assistive applications used by students with disabilities, they should have at least an awareness of what they are and of some simple online problems users might encounter.

Doing Good Work

Providing a more level learning space means giving motivated students with disabilities the opportunity to compete favorably with the rest of the class. It does not mean providing special treatment. In my teaching career, I have met students who consistently did poor work, offering one excuse after another—and some of these students have had disabilities. Often, they had previously been allowed to do sloppy work because of their disability. The teachers who did that did those students a disservice.

Once a student of mine who had a severe hearing impairment came to me seeking help. I extended myself to help her learn about learning and developing better study habits and writing skills. I also made it clear that she still had to successfully complete the assignments. She thanked me. Her public school teachers, she said, had felt sorry for her and "kindly" moved her along. She said it was the first time she had been forced to perform, and now knew that she really could succeed.

TAKE-AWAYS FROM THIS CHAPTER

In this chapter I outlined the three components of online accessibility for students with disabilities:

- The online learning interface or the courseware system must provide a gateway into the courses that can be navigated easily.

- The faculty needs to provide content that meets high standards of effective communication and avoids technical accessibility problems.

- The student has to come to the online learning experience prepared to be a responsible learner, including being equipped with a quality computer and adaptive technology to facilitate the online learning experience.

In the first two chapters of this book I sketched out a broad context in which to understand online learning accessibility. The goal is to provide you with a framework that will make your efforts to design accessible course content more meaningful. In subsequent chapters I focus on how to create effective and accessible online content and how to do it with techniques and strategies built into authoring tools with which you are already familiar.

Creating Accessible Content in Word and Excel

I n this chapter I focus primarily on using Microsoft Word to create accessible online course content—and to a lesser extent on Excel. The concepts outlined in this chapter will usually hold true for both the PC and Mac versions of the software, as well as for almost any modern, commercial word processing, or spreadsheet program. If you do not use Microsoft Office applications you probably use products that function in similar ways, so this chapter will nevertheless contain valuable information. Similarly, although the specific interface described is that of Word and Excel 2007, the same features are available to users of Office 2003, although the menu structure and option names may differ.

I discuss the formatting and other features that are built into Word and how to use them effectively to create accessible online content. I've also included some tips on which selections will support people with disabilities without compromising the document's appearance. Finally, I touch on simple things you can do to increase accessibility when using images, tables, and spreadsheets.

The information here is necessarily brief. Many extremely large books have been written on the capabilities of Word and Excel and similar programs. Likewise, a wealth of information is available online at Microsoft.com and other software vendors' Web sites. I urge you to explore these resources to learn ways of working more efficiently and improving the accessibility of your course content.

AN INTRODUCTION TO STRUCTURING DOCUMENTS IN WORD

At one time, users of personal computers were expected to use specialized applications to prepare different kinds of content. Something like Notepad was appropriate for simple, brief notes. For longer documents for which the author needed more control over formatting, WordPad or a similar program was helpful. You could build certain formatting into the text, and WordPad saved it in rich text format (RTF). Word processing programs, such as Microsoft Word, when they came along, had many, many more features to give authors control over their final product, so that it was almost ready for publishing. And over the years, word processing applications have accumulated richer feature sets that not only let users create content but also to output that content in many different document formats, such as HTML for Web pages.

We take this kind of "portability" for granted now, and the idea goes back many years, but it did not come about easily. Decades ago, there was a lot of discussion about what was called Standardized General Markup Language (SGML), which would have been a universal document standard, allowing text created in one word processor to be read by any other that used the standard. The commercial software companies, instead of building around a common markup language, however, opted for their own proprietary products, thus creating difficulties in sharing documents. Eventually the incompatibility problem was solved by the use of what is called a *style sheet* or *template* (depending on the program), which controls the way an entire document will be presented by almost any display technology that can interface with it. Style sheet features, correctly used, make a document more stable and consistent and guarantee that it can interface with other software—including the assistive technologies used by many people with disabilities.

Thanks to style sheets, making content accessible for students with disabilities can be quite simple. One basic content-authoring tool, such as Word, can be used to create online content that can then be posted into a learning management system. Even better, it can be posted as a Word document, a Web page, or a PDF document and maintain its original accessibility features across all three—so long as it was originally created with the universal design features built into the word processor.

CREATING WELL-STRUCTURED DOCUMENTS

As mentioned in Chapter Two, creating clearly written, modularized content is the first step toward assuring that content is accessible when it is put online. *Modularization,* or "chunking," includes using straightforward sentence structures, lists, relatively short paragraphs, and a hierarchy of headings to divide the content into logical, easily digested segments.

I cannot overemphasize the importance of careful planning before starting to write. As students, we were all taught to outline our papers before beginning to write, and we should adhere to that practice as instructors. Moreover, that outline should find its way onto the page in the form of headings. A well-structured document with clearly worded headings immediately communicates its content to everyone, including people with disabilities. The visible structure that headings provide helps the reader both navigate the content and more easily understand its meaning.

To illustrate: Before I gained access to content in an electronic form, I depended on someone reading to me for most of my information. However, often I was not sure of the meaning of what I was hearing. I knew that content was divided into topics by using paragraphs and headers, but the reader did not always convey that information to me clearly. If I understood what was being read as all being a continuation of the same content, I got one meaning one from it. However, if the content was divided up into several topics, even though the words were the same, the meaning could be quite different.

When you are reading a book or other material, you may not be consciously aware of the main heading or subheads. But whether you read a heading carefully or just run your eyes over it, it provides useful information. Well-written and well-designed headers serve as both summaries and signposts. They help you decide whether you're interested in reading the information that follows, tell you about the relationship (hierarchy) of information, help you find the parts that are relevant to you, and let you move around in the text quickly without becoming confused. They do a lot of work in a few words.

A simple example helps demonstrate the relationship between structure and meaning. In the following two columns, each list has the same text. Without any advance knowledge, the reader might assume the items in the left-hand list were cities. On the right, however, because of the structure—the formatting of the headings—it is clear that the items make up two lists of cities in two different states.

New York	**NEW YORK**
Albany	Albany
Buffalo	Buffalo
Washington	**WASHINGTON**
Spokane	Spokane
Seattle	Seattle

Readers of all types benefit from clearly structured documents, but it is especially important for some. People who are visual learners and those with visual processing disabilities benefit significantly when the heading structure supports the content's meaning and is clearly indicated in the layout of the content. Similarly, headings both help convey meaning and provide navigation assistance to anyone using screen reader software—so long as the headings have been coded, or *tagged*, appropriately, as discussed in the next section.

Using Microsoft Word's Styles to Show Structure

In a word processor, you have several options for formatting. You can select a portion of text and then individually select a typeface (e.g., Times Roman), font size, alignment, boldfacing, and other attributes to give it the appearance you want. However, a quicker and easier way to achieve the same result is to select a package of attributes, or a *style*, from Word 2007's Styles menu.

A style, in Word and other similar programs, is a set of commands that controls the appearance of the text it is applied to. In some instances, it also controls the function of that text within the document. The styles used in a document are contained in a separate file (called a *style sheet* or *template*) that travels with the document wherever it goes—including when the content is imported into a different type of software. These styles govern the appearance of the content whenever and wherever it is displayed.

Figure 3.1

How Three Different Header Levels Look Onscreen.

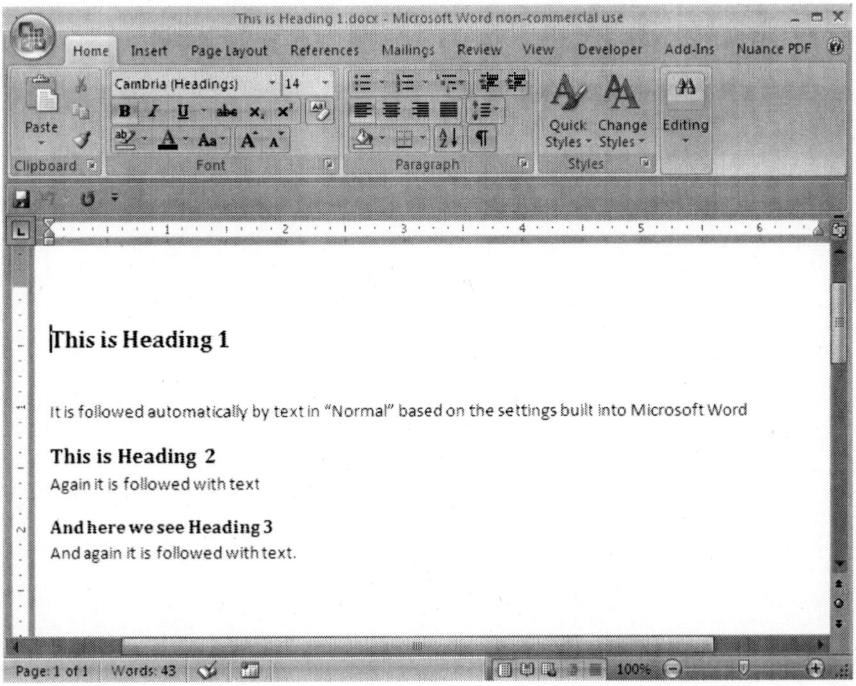

As mentioned, Word has a number of built-in heading styles. When you use them to structure a document, Word "understands" the structure—the hierarchy of the headings. That is, Word knows that Heading 2 text is subordinate to Heading 1, and Heading 3 is subordinate to Heading 2, because that information is included in the style along with the typeface, font size, and so forth. Figure 3.1 shows an example of three header levels.

However, if you create an identical heading by applying formatting manually, although it looks the same to you, the structural information is missing. For example, Figure 3.2 shows two lines of text, one formatted using the Heading 1 style and one formatted manually. Can you tell the difference? Of course not, but Word can.

Figure 3.2
The Same Text Formatted with a Style and Manually.

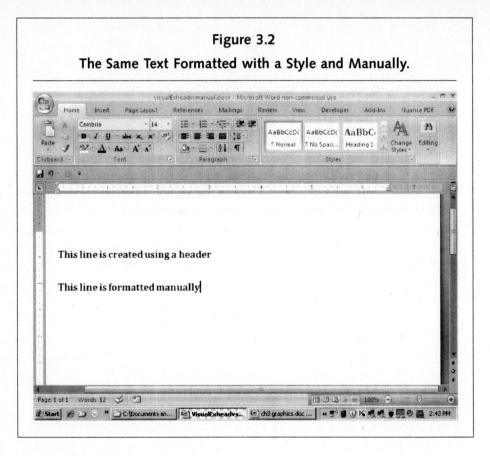

Why Use Styles?

The hidden information included in styles offers a wealth of benefits—for accessibility, of course, but also for automating a number of routine chores that can otherwise eat up far too much of your time and patience. Any document in Microsoft Word already has multiple styles connected with it, although most Word users are unaware of this fact. Word calls this collection of styles a template; some other programs use the term *style sheet.*

The default template, called Normal, has styles for different levels of headers, a Normal style for text paragraphs, and many more.

If you're like most people, you create your documents by using the features in the Format ribbon to create the appearance you want. Using styles—either those that are provided or new ones you create yourself—ensures a more consistent and professional-looking document, ultimately with less effort. For example, using styles can ensure that each heading at a particular level of hierarchy will be consistent, without your having to remember how you formatted the other ones. You just decide on the attributes you want, set them up *once* using dialog boxes you're already familiar with, and then apply that same formatting at will throughout the document.

Styles can be a very handy tool. The benefits include the ability to

- Create a consistent appearance throughout the document.
- Provide clear navigation for the reader of a document.
- Maintain the document structure and appearance wherever and whenever it is displayed, including when it is exported to a different document format.
- Automatically create a table of contents for the document that includes page numbers, hyperlinks, or both.
- Provide better accessibility to the document for readers with disabilities.

For the purpose of this book, I am, of course, most interested in persuading you to use styles because that way your documents will interface better with assistive technologies. However, the benefits of using styles are legion. For example, assuming styles have been applied consistently, an entire document can be reformatted with a few clicks, simply by changing the template, as shown in Figure 3.3.

Using Styles in Word 2007

Let's start with a simple exercise so you can see how easy it is to use styles to give a document structure:

1. Write four or more lines in Word. Limit the first three lines to only a few words long.
2. Now make the first line a main header. Locate the heading styles on the Styles ribbon (Figure 3.4) or menu (Figure 3.5), and select the Heading 1 style. In Word, you may also be able to achieve the same result by simultaneously pressing the CTRL, ALT, and 1 keys.
3. Repeat for the second line, but apply the Heading 2 style (CTRL-ALT-2).
4. Do the same for the third line but make it Heading 3 (CTRL-ALT-3).

Figure 3.3

The Same Document Formatted with Two Different Templates.

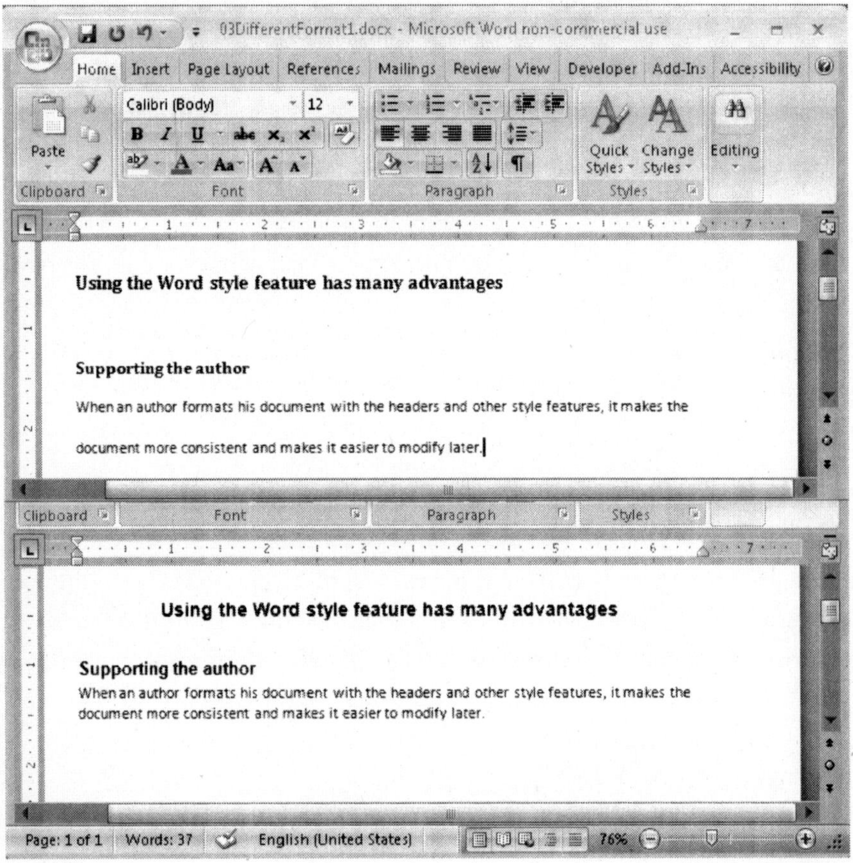

5. Leave the remaining line regular text. If you click on it, you should see that the default Normal style is applied. If it is not, for some reason, apply that style.

Customizing Styles

If you don't like the look of the headers you just created, that's easy to fix. You can select from dozens of font and alignment features and customize the format-

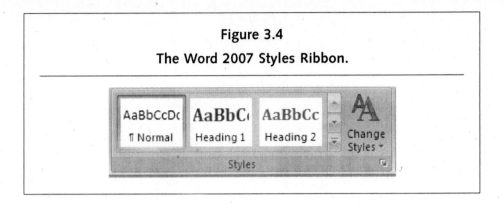

Figure 3.4

The Word 2007 Styles Ribbon.

ting to almost anything you desire. You can either change the attributes of the styles built into Word's Normal template, or you can create new styles (and templates) for different uses. The Styles ribbon shows the features you can define, which you are probably already familiar with: font type and size, boldfacing, italics, color, line spacing, and so on.

To modify an existing style in Word 2007:

1. Go to the Styles ribbon and click the arrow at the bottom right (see Figure 3.4).

2. Then select the style you want to change, and click the leftmost icon on the bottom of the Styles menu, as shown in Figure 3.5.

3. Enter the new formatting using the options provided, and save your changes.

Creating a Custom Style

You can create a new style in several ways. Here's an easy one:

1. Format a paragraph of text as you like.

2. Click anywhere in that paragraph, and then click the arrow at the bottom right of the Styles ribbon.

3. In the Styles menu, click the leftmost of the three icons at the bottom. You will see the dialog box shown in Figure 3.6.

4. Give the new style a name and select from the options at the bottom of the box:

Figure 3.5

Modifying the Heading 1 Style.

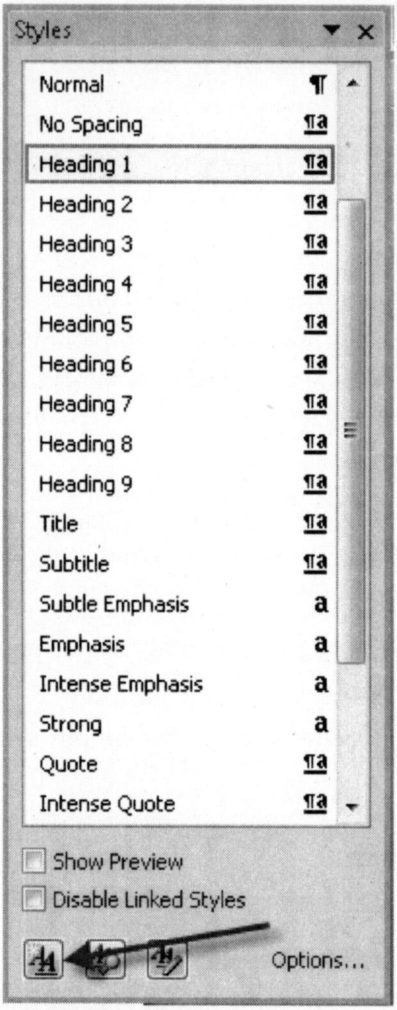

- Add to Quick Style List makes your new style readily accessible for reuse by adding it to the Styles ribbon, as shown in Figure 3.7.

- Add to Template makes the style available in any document that has the current template attached to it. For example, if your current document uses

Figure 3.6

Creating a New Style.

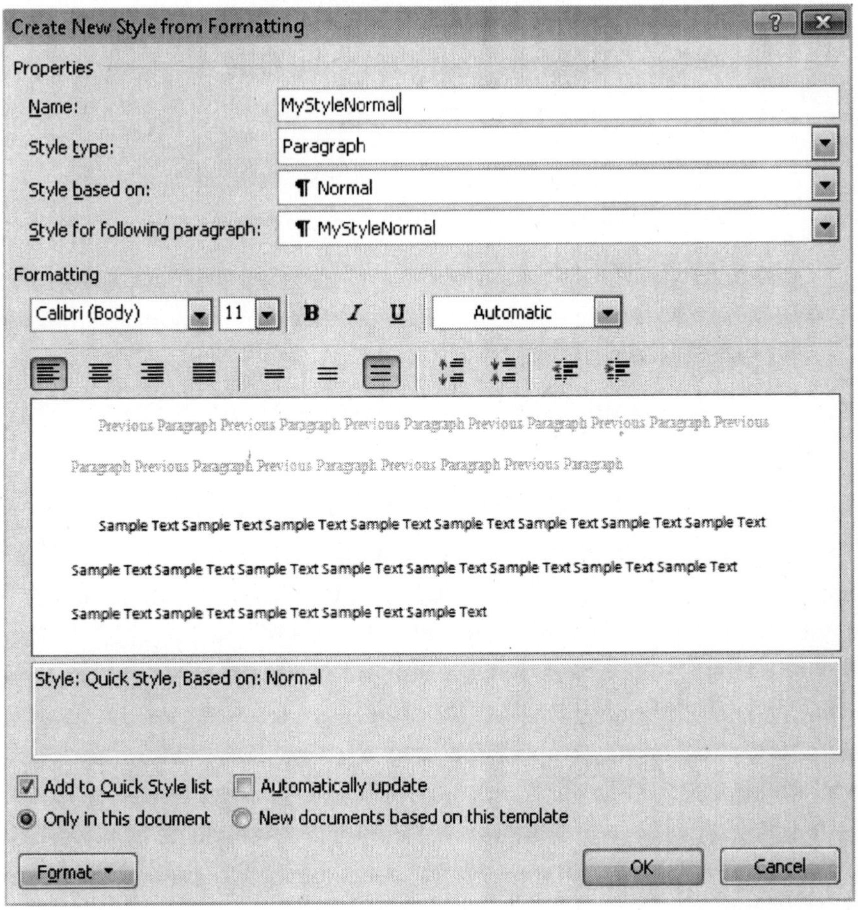

the default Normal template, any future document created from that template will automatically include the new style.

- Only in This Document restricts the style to the current document.

- Automatically Update does *not* mean that all text with that style will be updated when you make changes to the style (this is a common misconception). In fact, that behavior happens by default. Instead, Automatically

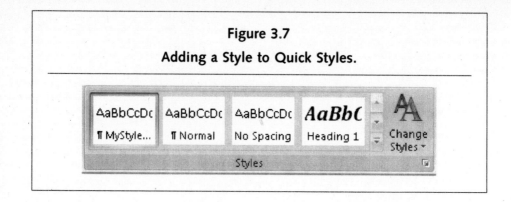

Figure 3.7

Adding a Style to Quick Styles.

Update changes *the style* whenever you reformat any text that is tagged with that style. Think long and hard before selecting this option, as it often has unexpected repercussions.

5. Click OK to add your style to the Styles list, as shown in Figure 3.8.

SELECTING STYLE ATTRIBUTES TO ENHANCE ACCESSIBILITY

In talking about people with disabilities, there is a tendency to oversimplify. Frequently, we are dealing with a mental image rather than with reality. I live next door to a large community of several thousand senior citizens. Canes, crutches, walkers, wheelchairs, hearing aids, and a dozen other similar devices abound. Most of these people will, at the same time, insist they are not "disabled." They have trouble getting around and need a walker, have trouble hearing and use a hearing aid, but they don't see themselves as having a disability. If, rather than thinking of ability and disability as either/or, we thought of them as the two ends of a single spectrum, then we would have a model that comes closer to mirroring reality.

Similarly, when we think about how to improve a document's accessibility or usability for people with disabilities, it is important to realize that not only are there different disabilities but that even within a single disability group each person is unique. In terms of document design, this means there is no simple list of fonts and colors that can be memorized and applied. Since the goal of good design and layout is to provide clues that help communicate the content to the user, designers need a general overview of the issues—the big picture. After that, deciding on exact formatting is more art than science.

Figure 3.8

The Styles List with a New Style Added.

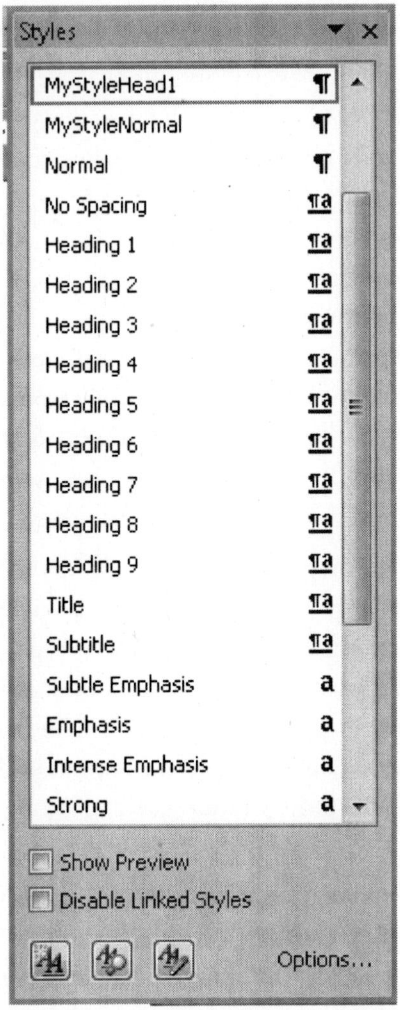

Here are some issues to consider in designing an accessible document in Word. Although the basic structural features, specifically the heading hierarchy, are exported along with the text, specific formatting features may be altered, especially when documents are uploaded to a learning management system. This means you need to check the final output against this list and have the necessary changes made for anything that doesn't conform to these broad guidelines:

- *Typeface:* Using an ornate font is never a good idea for online materials, regardless of who the audience is. A simple, crisp font requires less visual processing to understand, which means sans serif fonts such as Verdana are the safer choice.

- *Font size:* Typically, font size will vary depending on the purpose of the text. Headings should be more prominent than body copy, and higher-level headings are typically larger than lower-level ones. Beyond that, there are a number of variables. The same size type in different fonts can look considerably different and actually take up more (or less) space. In general, for body text, 10- to 12-point type is the norm. You should definitely avoid using something like the small print at the bottom of a insurance policy, but you don't want your text to look like it's for a beginning reader. It is fair to assume that users with more severe visual limitations will be using screen magnification software, so there's no need to enlarge the type for them.

- *Color:* As discussed in Chapter Two, color alone should not be used to convey information, as some colors cannot be distinguished by people who are color blind. That doesn't mean you can't use colored type, just that any information coded by color should also be indicated in another way. On the overall design front, the most important accessibility issue involving color is having distinct enough contrast between the background and the text and avoiding a background (such as pure white) that can create glare on a computer monitor.

- *Line spacing:* People who do not have trouble actually seeing text but who have problems visually processing information benefit from more blank space on a page. Using line and a half spacing may enable these people to decode the information better. However, double spacing is probably a look most authors would rather avoid.

- *Line length:* Some readers with learning disabilities have trouble tracking long lines—as do many people without disabilities. Appropriate line length (online or in print) is related to both font size and line spacing, and any designer worth his or her salt will be aware of these relationships.

CREATING A TABLE OF CONTENTS

As discussed earlier in the chapter, straightforward writing, clear structure indicated by meaningful headers, and text that is divided into small, manageable chunks will help all students grasp and understand the content you provide. Another aid that can be very useful with longer documents is a table of contents. A contents list can help with both document navigation and understanding the content. (Remember that document navigation is included in both the Section 508 standards and the WCAG Version 2 guidelines.)

Word has a tool that enables you to automatically generate a table of contents. For a paper document or PDF, it will automatically put in the correct page numbers for each heading you include in the contents. If the document will be distributed electronically (in either HTML or PDF format), each entry in the table of contents can be linked to the corresponding section in the electronic document. The contents are exported with the document as it is repurposed from Word to the Web.

Assuming your document has been structured properly using heading styles (this is essential!), the word processor can make a table of contents for you in a matter of seconds:

1. Create a blank line where you want the table of contents to appear, near the beginning of the document, and leave your cursor there.
2. In Word 2007, go to the Reference ribbon and select Table of Contents, as shown in Figure 3.9.

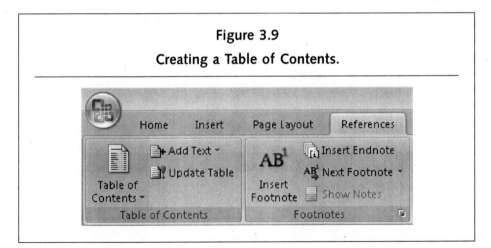

Figure 3.9

Creating a Table of Contents.

3. Word's built-in table of contents offers a variety of options, as shown in Figure 3.10. For electronic text, you can set up your contents so that each heading entry in the electronic text is a link, or for a paper document you can have it list page numbers. In the Word document, entries in the contents are linked to the headings in the body, and if you create a PDF from your "paper" document, the entries can also be linked in the final document.

The ability to click on an entry in a table of contents and immediately jump to that topic is an aid for everyone, but even more so for users with disabilities, since it eliminates the effort of having to skim to locate the desired content. Skimming or paging through a document, though easy (if tedious) for people without disabilities, can be stressful for someone with difficulty visually processing information or someone who has a motor impairment.

MAKING IMAGES IN WORD ACCESSIBLE

You can include images in your course content and still have that content be accessible to someone who cannot see but who is using screen reader software by your adding an alternative description, as discussed in Chapter Two. Adding an image to a text document is simple. You can either copy and paste the image into your document, or you can use the menu option for inserting an image, navigate to the picture file that you want to use, and then click a button to finish.

Once you've inserted the image, you add the alt text to make sure it's accessible as follows:

1. In Word 2007, start by right-clicking on the image.
2. Select the Format Picture option, and click the Alt Text tab, as shown in Figure 3.11.
3. Type in your description or label and click the Close button. Now anyone using a screen reader will hear that label when they come to the picture in the document, and other users will see that label when they move their pointer over the image.

But, you may be wondering, what kind of alternative text would be appropriate? In general, the shortest descriptive label is best. For example, if you have a

Figure 3.10

Configuring Your Table of Contents.

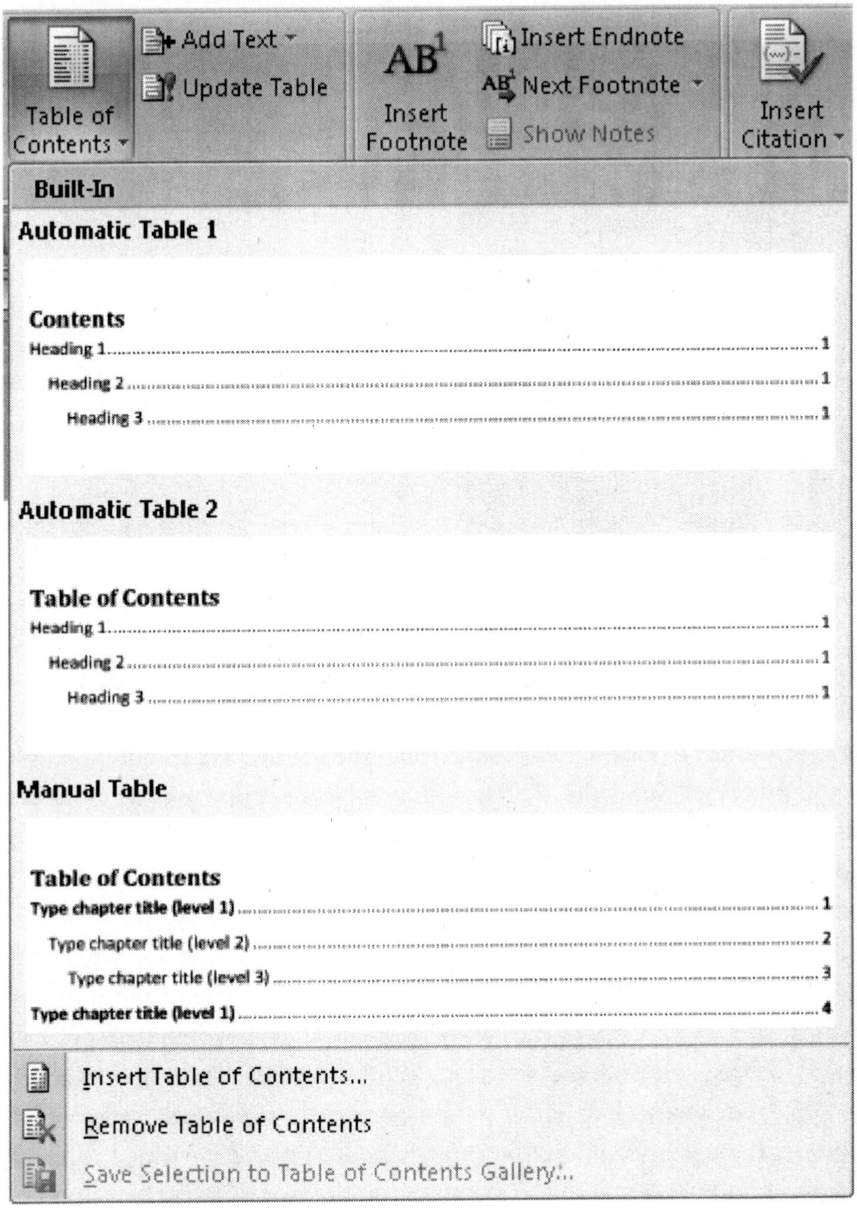

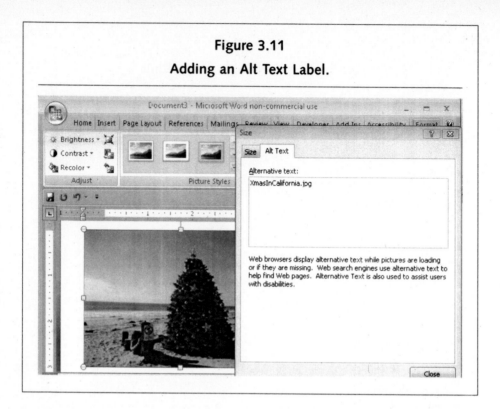

Figure 3.11

Adding an Alt Text Label.

snapshot of a person, "Photo of Joe Smith" would be adequate. If a fuller description is needed, try to keep it brief.

As mentioned in Chapter Two, sometimes the Alt Text tag should be empty—but you should still have one. If an image doesn't convey any content information and is included primarily to add visual interest, then someone using a screen reader might prefer not to be distracted by it. In this case, use the *null alt text attribute:* just put a space in the Alt Text field. This tells the screen reader to ignore the figure. If instead, you omit the Alt Text attribute altogether, the screen reader tells the reader there is an image but, frustratingly, has no description to offer.

Sometimes, of course, a picture demands a longer explanation than just a short label. If you have, for example, a drawing of an electronic circuit in an electronics class, the issue is very different. If the image conveys significant, complex information, just a name would not be enough description. If the image is complex, it may be a good idea to provide an explanation as part of the text preceding the graphic. This will help all users understand the full meaning you intend to communicate. In such a situation, you might also need to provide a student who is blind with a tactile, raised-line drawing, as discussed in Chapter Six.

Bear in mind that pictures often contain words, but a screen reader cannot recognize that part of the image as text and will not read it. Some banners, for example, are graphics that consist entirely of words, but to a computer and screen reader, it's just a picture. Be sure to repeat any relevant words in the Alt Text field.

CREATING WORD TABLES AND EXCEL SPREADSHEETS

Tables and spreadsheets are similar. The main difference between a table in Word and a spreadsheet in Excel is that the spreadsheet has much more functionality. But as representations of data, they have much in common, in that the information is displayed in a format that depends on a visual layout.

As discussed in Chapter Two, tables and spreadsheets can pose problems for students with some disabilities. This means that clarity and simplicity in tables is key. The more columns and rows, the more difficult the table becomes to comprehend. When you have a lot of information that is best displayed in tabular format, an Excel spreadsheet may be a better tool than a table in a Word document because Excel spreadsheets interface better with screen readers than do Word tables.

You can help students with learning disabilities who may have trouble decoding or understanding densely formatted information, such as that in a table, by including a text explanation of the table or spreadsheet that makes it clear what you want the reader to learn. This way, the student has two different views of the information, which reinforce each other. Remember, just because the meaning of something is clear to you doesn't mean it will be as clear to someone else.

When providing such an additional text description of table information, you might want to spell out numbers instead of using numerals. This will be helpful to people with the learning disability known as *dysnumeria*, which means their brain scrambles the order of numbers.

Finally, avoid using empty rows or columns to provide visual separations between cells. Both Word and Excel offer other ways to format cells so as to provide white space. I urge you to learn and use these tools. For someone using a screen reader, moving cell by cell down a column or across a row when it has been left empty for visual effect is needlessly time consuming—and therefore quite annoying.

Using Word Tables

To create a table in Word 2007:

1. Select Table from the Insert ribbon, as shown in Figure 3.12.

2. Pick the number of columns and rows you want.

3. Click Insert Table, and Word will set up a table with those dimensions, ready for you to use.

As discussed in Chapter Two, the content of a table's cells usually only makes sense in relationship to the row and column headers. Anyone seeing the simple table on page 53 as a whole will readily understand the amounts in their context and will quickly recognize which column has the row headers and which row has the column headers. For someone using a screen reader, each individual cell's

Figure 3.12

Inserting a Table.

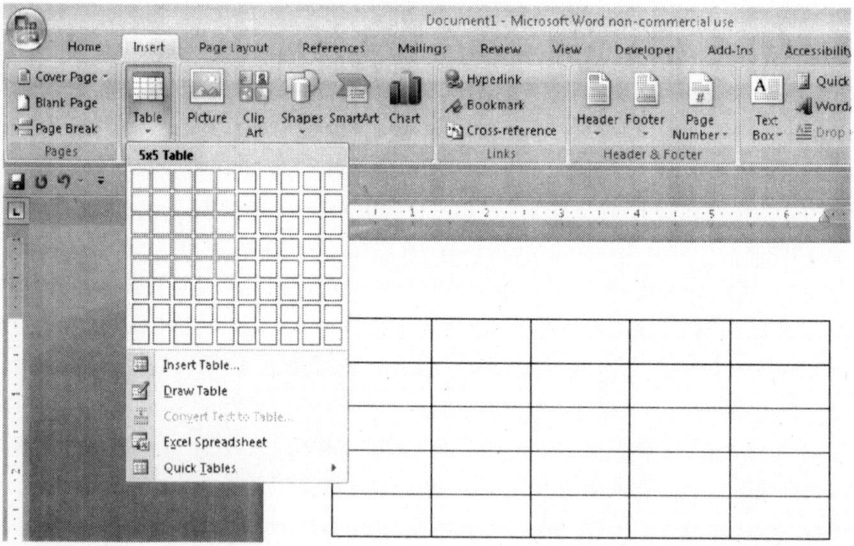

contents is discrete, but that person will also quickly recognize the headers and, because the table is so small, could even memorize them enough to recall and relate the correct header with the individual cells. However, if there were eight or nine rows and just as many columns, the person would undoubtedly become confused about which header was the relevant one for any individual cell, and the table's meaning would quickly get lost in a mental fog. Large tables can also be problematic for people with learning disabilities and users of screen magnification devices.

EXPENSES	BREAKFAST	LUNCH	DINNER
Tuesday	$9.95	$12.23	$25.12
Wednesday	$5.95	$7.29	$21.12
Thursday	$11.95	$5.99	$19.21

This is an example in which accessibility is jointly determined by the content creator and the user's skill with his or her assistive software. The JAWS screen reader and similar sophisticated software permit the user to set marks to indicate which row has the column headers and which column has the row headers. Then, using that information, the synthesizer can—instead of reading just a cell's content—read the relevant header first, and then the cell information. This is precisely what someone with normal vision is doing as the eye quickly scans the table, relating the cell to its relevant headers.

When using tables in documents, you can help users of screen readers in two ways. First, as mentioned above, preface the table with a brief summary of what it means; this will also assist the rest of your readers. Second, as part of that description, identify which row and column contain the headers; this will help screen reader users set up their software to speak the relevant header along with the contents of a cell.

Making Excel Spreadsheets More Accessible

Spreadsheets, like tables, provide an excellent visual way to organize related but discrete bits of information and permit the reader to understand and analyze that data in different ways. Users can manipulate and analyze a spreadsheet's content, however, assuming they have the requisite skills.

As with Word tables, it's important to provide some explanation of the spreadsheet so that users can immediately view it in a meaningful context, and they may also benefit from being told which row and column contain the relevant headers. Excel makes the latter job easier, as the software itself can identify the header row and column. Used correctly, this capability will enable screen readers to automatically speak the row and column headings as the user moves between cells.

To tag your headers in Excel 2007:

If row 1 and column A contain headers, you would put your cursor in the top left cell, A1.

1. Select the Formulas tab of the ribbon, and then select the Name Manager, as shown in Figure 3.13.

2. Click the New button and type in the word "Title." This tells the screen reader that row 1 contains column headers and column 1 contains row headers.

Figure 3.13

Tagging Headings in Excel.

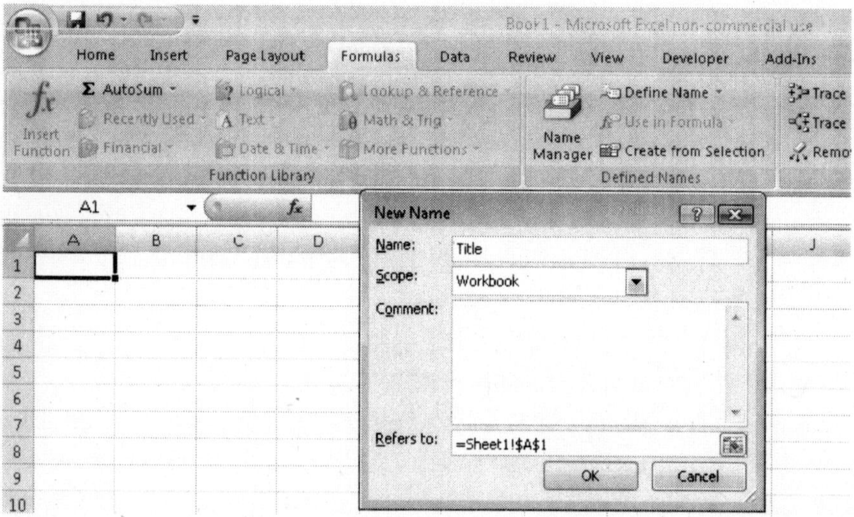

3. If your headers are not in column A and row 1, instead of putting the cursor in A1, place it in the first cell in the column that contains a row header, and enter "RowTitle" as the name.

4. Repeat step 3 using the first cell in the row that contains column headers, but enter the name "ColumnTitle."

Screen readers recognize the Title, RowTitle, and ColumnTitle names, so as a screen reader's focus moves from cell to cell, it will first speak the relevant header, then the cell coordinates, and finally its contents.

These are only a few simple things that you, as an author, can do to make it easier for a student using adaptive technology to access a spreadsheet. The more spreadsheet skills that you and the student have, the better use you both will be able to make of this technology.

TAKE-AWAYS FROM THIS CHAPTER

Although this discussion has gone into some detail on how to accomplish increased accessibility by using a few standard features of Word and Excel, there are really only a handful of things to learn and keep in mind. For most course content, these are the features to remember:

- Structure the document thoughtfully.
- Use Word styles to implement that structure.
- Add Alt Text labels to identify images.
- For complex graphics, include a discussion explaining them in the text.
- Keep tables and spreadsheets simple, make headers clear, and include a text summary.

Creating Accessible Presentations with PowerPoint

In the previous chapter, I described how using some of the features in Microsoft Word can separate the content from how it is presented, which allows the document to be displayed in other file types without losing its basic structural features. In this chapter I discuss how to use similar features in PowerPoint so that its basic structure and the organization of the document's content will be preserved when it is repurposed as a Word or a PDF document, printed out as a lecture handout, or posted online in HTML on a Web page. More important for the purposes of this book, software used by people with disabilities can access the formatting information and use it to help readers improve their understanding of the document's content.

POWERPOINT AND UNIVERSAL DESIGN

As you'll recall from Chapter Two, universal design means creating things so that they will be easily usable by a very wide range of people and interface with a number of different systems. In our context, universal design has two meanings:

- The information should be understandable by all (or at least most) people.
- The content will be fully accessible from a number of different technology platforms.

Universal Design Under the Hood

Often, authoring tools such as PowerPoint provide multiple ways to produce the layout and appearance you want. Although the different methods may create results that *look* the same, "under the hood" they may be significantly different.

A simple example would be creating two columns of text. You can do this by lining up the content vertically by using tabs or the space bar. Visually, *you* would see two columns, but what the technology sees is a line of text with tab spaces, or both—not columns. However, PowerPoint also has a tool that lets you automatically set up two columns and controls the spacing and appearance for you.

Using the second option is almost certainly less tedious for the author and will give a more consistent appearance, but it can also help people with disabilities because their assistive software will understand that the text is formatted in columns. For example, screen reader software would know that the text in each column should be read as a unit, and would therefore read column one continuously from top to bottom, and then move onto column two, instead of reading across the page. A screen magnification program would also recognize that there were two columns and could display them one at a time. In both cases, the software is doing what another user's eye would do automatically.

Whenever an authoring tool has a feature that will set up the layout and appearance for you, learn and use that feature instead of trying to approximate the same thing manually. You'll be doing yourself a favor, as well as benefiting everyone who reads the document, since these tools create a more consistent and attractive appearance. Further, as we have discussed, for students using assistive technologies, your use of these tools can mean they are better able to access your contents and understand it more easily and fully. Finally, proper use of formatting features will ensure that the document carries the page layout information with it when you export, or *repurpose,* the content to another format. This saves you effort down the line and ensures that readers of the repurposed content see what you intended they should see.

Universal Design On-Screen

Keeping in mind the behind-the-scenes features that provide the more general structural aspects of the page, let's turn our attention to the visual aspects of designing a PowerPoint presentation. Most of the concepts discussed in the chapter on Word will apply here, as well as a few that are specific to slide shows:

- Use a simple slide layout.

- Organize content in a logical structure.

- Use simple language that avoids ambiguity and needless complexity.

- Watch out for excessive brevity. On slides there can be a tendency to be so concise that the meaning becomes obscure. Be sure you're being clear—don't cut necessary words just to make things fit.

- Make sure every item in the presentation keeps the focus and helps move the content forward.

- Use legible type. It is difficult to specify a font size to use, as what is best will depend on how and where the slides are viewed. PowerPoint's built-in templates and format generally work best for slide shows. Verdana or another sans serif typeface is a good choice for legibility.

- Be sure the contrast between background and foreground color is good. Dark type on a light background or vice versa is best.

- Leave ample white space. If the content is packed too densely, reading the slide during a presentation may take more concentration than most people possess.

The Pros and Cons of PowerPoint's "Bells and Whistles"

PowerPoint includes a vast array of features that can add sparkle to a presentation and make it far more interesting and entertaining than content designed in a word processor. We live in a fast-paced world nowadays and are accustomed to professionally produced television and online content. When course content can productively utilize graphics, sound, music, animation, or video, the audience will be more engaged and less apt to become bored and lose focus. Even better, perhaps, is the ability of these enrichments to appeal to the different needs of text-oriented learners, visual learners, and auditory learners—and to engage them. The ability to deliver content in multiple modes means that no learner group needs to be excluded. Offering content in more than one mode can also provide reinforcement, which helps with learning.

But all these benefits come with a caveat: the same features that entertain and engage can also distract and interfere with the student grasping the *relevant* content. The bottom line is, don't add features for their own sake. If you're adding features to help gain the student's attention, be sure that each feature also supports the content—otherwise it may simply become a distraction.

DESIGNING ACCESSIBLE POWERPOINT PRESENTATIONS

PowerPoint presentations can be made available online in a variety of formats. They may be converted to Web (HTML) pages, they can made into PDF documents that can be accessed online or downloaded, or the actual PowerPoint slide show can be offered as a downloadable file, in which case users will need to have PowerPoint or a PowerPoint viewer on their computer. This range of formats means I have to discuss two aspects of the PowerPoint application. First, I look at how assistive technologies interface with PowerPoint to provide access for users with disabilities. Second, I discuss what you can do in designing the PowerPoint presentations to further facilitate accessibility.

Accessibility Issues

The accessibility issues related to PowerPoint for people with different disabilities fall into two categories: navigation and comprehension. Users must be able to move through the presentation, and they must be able to perceive the slides and understand their meaning.

PowerPoint presentations, including most of their basic features, interface reasonably well with the major commercial assistive technology applications, including onscreen keyboard software, voice recognition programs, screen magnification software, and screen reading software.

These applications impact the major disability groups described in earlier chapters:

- Users with upper body limitations who cannot use a mouse can use either an onscreen keyboard or voice recognition to control the slide show.

- Users with limited vision can use screen magnification software to magnify the slides as necessary.

- Users with learning disabilities who have problems deciphering the text on a slide can also use screen magnification to limit the amount of text that is visible at one time.

- Users who are blind can use screen reader software along with the space bar on the keyboard to move through the presentation, and the software's synthesizer will vocalize the text on the slides as well as speak any Alt Text identifying images.

The one area where these applications will not help is audio. For users who have severe hearing impairments, presentations that rely on audio narration can be problematic. I provide solutions for this problem briefly later in this chapter, in the section on creating narrated slide shows, and in more detail in the chapter on multimedia (Chapter Seven), in which I discuss captioning in some detail.

Distribution Formats

As mentioned earlier, presentations created in PowerPoint can be distributed in any of several different formats:

- PowerPoint (.ppt or .pptx file)
- Narrated PowerPoint (.pts or .pxs file)
- Word
- PDF
- HTML
- Hard copy

Exporting or repurposing PowerPoint files (as well as Word and Excel documents) for distribution online and elsewhere is not difficult. However, the variety of formats and distribution options means that the topic requires a separate, more detailed description, which I provide in Chapter Five. For the purposes of this chapter, the important thing is to learn how to build accessibility features into your PowerPoint slide shows. Although not all of these features will always carry through in the repurposed version, including them in your design is a good habit to form. In the discussion that follows, when an accessibility feature will not export with the presentation, it will be noted and an alternative solution suggested.

Slide Layout

PowerPoint 2007 provides several built-in slide layouts, as shown in Figure 4.1. (You can also create your own custom layouts, but doing so is beyond the scope of this book.) The layout options are located on the Home tab, in the Slide group.

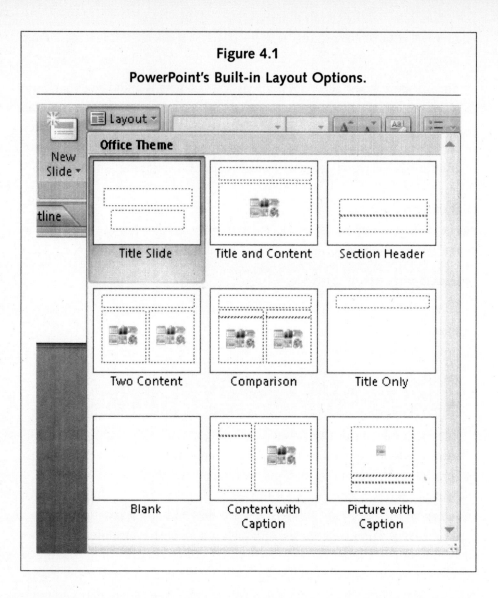

Figure 4.1

PowerPoint's Built-in Layout Options.

When you create a new presentation, by default the first slide is the Title slide, which has placeholders for a title and subtitle, as shown in Figure 4.2. The layout that will automatically be inserted next is called Title and Content (see Figure 4.3); it is what most people picture when they think of a PowerPoint slide. For that reason, users with disabilities will find this familiar and easy to understand.

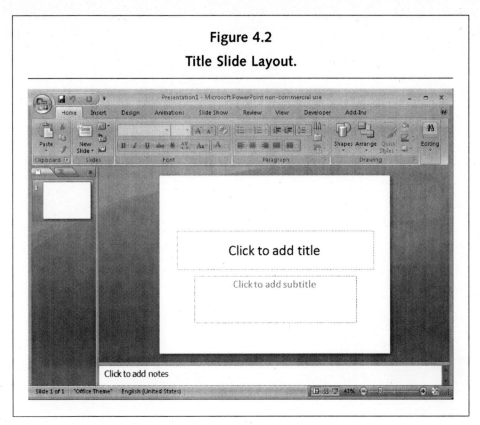

Figure 4.2

Title Slide Layout.

Colors and Fonts

The importance of having good contrast between foreground and background colors cannot be overemphasized. Both the colors themselves and their lightness and darkness values need to contrast.

PowerPoint presenters often tend to get a bit carried away with demonstrating their creativity. They want to present something that is different and catches the attention of the viewer—and there's nothing wrong with that. But it is important that the design not distract from the content and not create problems in understanding what the slide is trying to say (see Figure 4.4 for an example).

PowerPoint gives you the ability to customize your slides' appearance in almost any way you can imagine, but playing it safe may be a better bet. Wide selections of designs or "themes" are built into the program, and most presenters will select one of these rather than designing their own from scratch. Before

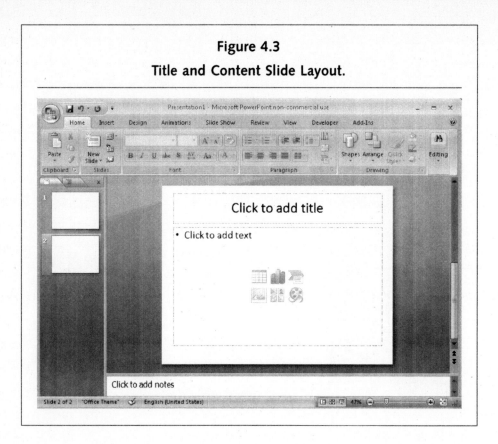

Figure 4.3

Title and Content Slide Layout.

selecting one, consider carefully how clear, uncluttered, and easy it is to read. Some focus more on being unique and eye-catching than on good design. To see what's on offer, go to the Design tab and select the Themes group.

PowerPoint Slide Font Size

The default font sizes set up in PowerPoint will generally work well. If you really need to squeeze more information on the slide, you can make the font a little smaller, but beware because that will cause problems if you shrink it too much. Users with very poor vision will be using screen magnification software, and they should be able to magnify the content to compensate for the smaller font. However, someone with only minor vision impairment may not use special software, so shrinking the font could be problematic. Users with learning disabilities may also have a problem because the content has become more dense and harder

Figure 4.4

A Slide with Poor Contrast.

to decode. There is no hard and fast rule—it's a judgment call—but if you find you need to reduce the body text to less than about 12 points to get it to fit, consider splitting the text between two slides.

Pictures and Other Graphics

Like Word, PowerPoint will allow you to add a descriptive Alt Text tag to an image; the procedure is the same in both applications (see "Making Images in Word Accessible" in Chapter Three). If the graphic is merely decorative, putting a space into the Alt Text field, making it a Null Alt Text tag, is appropriate. Conversely, if the image is complex and requires a longer description, you may need to add a longer description in the notes area of the slide. In that case, use the Alt Text tag for the image to tell screen reader users to look at the slide notes.

Tables

Although it is possible to make a table on a PowerPoint slide, the size of a slide limits how large the table can be. However, this limitation is beneficial for viewers with disabilities. As discussed in earlier chapters, users with visual processing disabilities will, in most cases, be able to decode a small table. Those using screen magnification to view the slide show will find a small table less confusing too.

Users who are blind and rely on a screen reader will not be able to understand PowerPoint tables as well as they will a spreadsheet, because the screen reader will not be able to help the user by associating each cell with the appropriate header. Yet because these tables will be small, these users should still be able to understand them without that assistance.

Features to Avoid

The features described below are problematic for various reasons, including a user with an older version of the assistive software. Although new assistive technologies may interact with these items in the future, for now, avoid using the following:

- *Text boxes*

  PowerPoint authors sometimes use text boxes instead of the content area provided in the built-in layouts to put text on a slide. When the presentation is exported to another format, text boxes often get lost. This is clearly a problem for all users—not just those with disabilities.

- *Animations*

  Authors are often attracted by the ability to use animations in PowerPoint presentations, but these are also lost when the presentation is repurposed. Furthermore, even in the native PowerPoint format animations can confuse users with learning disabilities, and animations can actually cause screen readers to crash.

- *Slide transitions*

  Wipes, fades, and other slide transitions cause problems similar to animations. Remember, it's best to err on the side of simplicity when there's any doubt.

- *Automatic timing*

  PowerPoint allows you to preset the interval until the next slide is displayed and thus create slide shows that run by themselves. Even users without disabilities may not be comfortable with the slide timings you set. Let the reader decide the pace.

- *Hyperlinks and buttons*

  Embedded hyperlinks do not work with screen reading software, and this has continued to be true over several generations of PowerPoint. If a hyperlink is intended to let the user play a multimedia presentation that accompanies the presentation, instead of placing a link or button on the slide, have the media play automatically when the slide opens instead.

CREATING NARRATED SLIDE SHOWS

Different people design and use PowerPoint presentations in different ways, but in general slide shows present only the outline of a topic. When the show is delivered to a live audience, the presenter fleshes out that outline with a longer lecture. A narrated PowerPoint presentation simulates this situation. A recorded audio narration is attached to each slide, expanding on its content.

Accessibility Issues

Except for those who have hearing impairments, narrated presentations will present few problems for these disability groups:

- People with motor impairments will not have any problems using their assistive technology to operate the presentation, and their impairment will not interfere with their viewing the slides.

- People with low vision should have no real problems controlling the presentation or seeing what is on the slides.

- People with learning disabilities should have no problem and, in fact, will benefit from receiving content in two sensory modes.

- People who are blind will be able to listen to the narration and have the screen reader vocalize the slide contents. However, there is a problem for users who are blind *accessing* a narrated PowerPoint. People who can see can usually process the visual and audio content of slides simultaneously, with little problem; in contrast, the person who is blind will hear the narration and the synthetic voice reading the slide contents simultaneously. It is more difficult to separate two content streams when they are in a single sensory mode. Most users will probably try to focus on what the narrator is saying and may miss some of the slide's content. For that reason, it's important to thoroughly discuss the slide's contents in the narration, so that the listener will not miss anything important. The other solution is for the person who is blind to silence the screen reader while listening to the presenter and, then, before going to the next slide to use the screen reader to examine the slide contents before continuing.

- People with hearing impairments are the one group who will have serious problems because of the audio in the narration; the solution is to include a transcript of the narration, as discussed below.

What You Will Need Before Making the Narration

Before you start recording, you need to be sure you're properly equipped and set up. This includes having

- A completed set of PowerPoint slides.
- An outline of what you will say or, even better, an actual script.
- A location where you can make a recording without being disturbed. (Unplug or turn off your phone. Let others know not to disturb you. Select a room that does not create an echo and where there is no outside or background noise.)
- A dependable microphone. Unless you are also recording music, you only need a microphone suitable for voice dictation. Select a mic that is good for middle range sounds and that will exclude ambient noise.

Adding the Narration

Use these steps to add narration to a slide show:

1. Have the slide show you want to narrate open in PowerPoint. Then, as shown in Figure 4.5, click the Slide Show tab, and then click Record Narration.

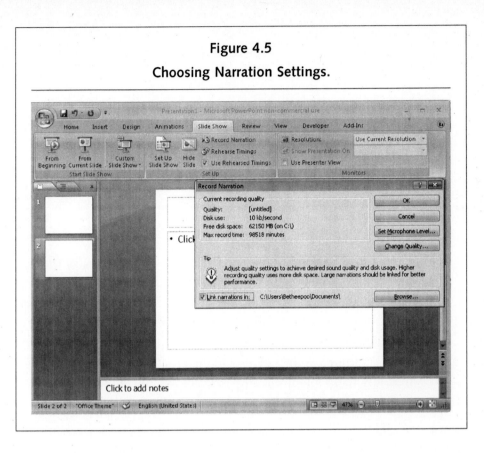

Figure 4.5

Choosing Narration Settings.

2. Click on Set Microphone Level, and speak into the microphone. You will see a sound bar that moves as you talk, and PowerPoint will automatically select the right volume setting.

3. Check the "Link narrations in" box, and be sure that the Browse field is pointing to the folder where your PowerPoint presentation is stored. This saves the narration sound files in that same directory.

4. Click OK to close the dialog box. As soon as you do, the first slide in your presentation appears in Slide Show mode and PowerPoint starts to record your audio.

5. When you are ready to discuss the second slide, use the space bar to advance the slide show, and continue your narration. When you have finished the narration for the last slide, press the space bar once more.

Figure 4.6
Saving the Narration.

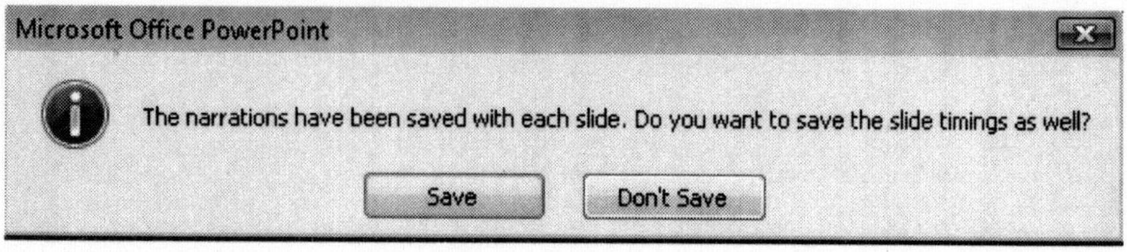

Microsoft Office PowerPoint

The narrations have been saved with each slide. Do you want to save the slide timings as well?

[Save] [Don't Save]

6. Slide Show mode closes and you are presented with the choice of whether to save the slide timings with the presentation, as shown in Figure 4.6. If you save the settings, the narrated PowerPoint with its audio will progress automatically from slide to slide. However, as stated earlier, I strongly recommend *not* saving them, so that the person viewing the narrated slide show can control when the slides—and their narration—advance. This has obvious advantages for anyone who wants to carefully study the content of the presentation, as well as for people with disabilities.

Note: An application called LecShare Pro provides an alternate way to record audio for online PowerPoint slide shows, among its other capabilities. If you'll be posting slide shows online, rather than distributing them in some other way, you might want to explore this option. Trial and other versions can be downloaded from www.lecshare.com. LecShare is discussed in more detail in Chapter Five.

Captioning a Narrated Slide Show

There is no simple way to provide captioning for users with hearing impairments within a narrated PowerPoint show. However, one work-around is to add a transcript of the narration in the notes area of an unnarrated version of the presentation. You can then publish the file to Word, and select the option to include both notes and slide. This way, the hearing impaired person can have a handout that shows the slide image along with the text of the narration. This method is explained in more detail in Chapter Five.

Adding actual captions to a slide show is covered in Chapter Seven, on multimedia.

TAKE-AWAYS FROM THIS CHAPTER

Although this discussion of PowerPoint has gone into some detail on how to increase the accessibility of PowerPoint presentations by using a few standard features (and avoiding a few others), there are really only a handful of things you should learn and keep in mind:

- Structure the presentation thoughtfully.
- Select contrasting foreground and background colors.
- Don't overcrowd your slides. Keep the content easy to read.
- Use a clean typeface and an adequate font size.
- Avoid using text boxes.
- Add alt text labels to identify images.
- Avoid using animations, slide transitions, and automatic timing.
- For complex graphics or tables, include a longer explanation in the slide notes.
- Provide a transcript of narration for those who will be unable to hear the audio.

PowerPoint presentations can be delivered in many forms to suit many diverse situations. In the next chapter I explore how that can be done in such a way that the content remains accessible no matter how and where it is distributed.

Delivering Accessible Content

Once you have created accessible documents in a Microsoft Office (or similar) application, you are ready to provide this course content to students. Because of the versatility of the Office applications, you have a wide variety of options. You can put it on the Web, upload it to a learning management system, e-mail it, and more. You can also provide it in any of several different file formats. If your class meets in person part of the time, you may hand the content to students on a CD-ROM or USB storage device. You might even hand the students in your classroom hard copies of the item, in which case you might even occasionally need to provide a hard-copy embossed Braille version for students who are blind.

This chapter covers how to take your accessible Office content and deliver it in a wide variety of settings and in a diverse set of file types while still maintaining its accessibility. Distributing content created in Word, Excel, and PowerPoint, respectively, is covered first, followed by using a number of third-party tools for verifying the accessibility of content, either before or after it is posted online.

A WORD ABOUT FILE TYPES

In general, if you will be distributing Office files in "native" file formats such as .doc and .xls, be aware that 2003 versions of Office applications cannot read the

Office 2007 file formats (.docx, .xlsx, .pptx) unless the user has installed a file converter. The free Office 2007-to-2003 converter is available by download from Microsoft, but not all features translate from 2007 to 2003. You will be doing your students a favor if you save any native-format documents in Office 2003 format.

Because we are focusing on providing accessible content for students with disabilities, you may be looking for advice as to which file types are best. When faculty post content into their college's learning management system it is common to provide the native Word or PowerPoint file. It is also common to provide the content as Web pages. If the content was designed using the guidelines provided in the previous two chapters, the native formats should meet the students' needs.

Later in this chapter I touch on how to turn native file content into accessible Web pages. However, this still leaves a number of other file types that can be exported from Word and PowerPoint. While those formats may be used less frequently, in some cases they may either meet your needs or help with a particular student's problem, so I discuss other formats briefly as well.

DISTRIBUTING ACCESSIBLE WORD DOCUMENTS

Microsoft Word gives you a wide range of options for saving a document, as shown in Figure 5.1. Which option you choose depends on how you will ultimately be distributing the document, as described next.

Native File Formats: .doc and .docx

Documents in Word's native file format (preferably .doc, as mentioned above) can be posted for download on an FTP site or Web page or distributed to students by e-mail. If you are working with a learning management system, you can also upload a .doc or .docx document to the LMS so that it can be read online. In this situation, the system will usually repurpose the document into a Web page.

Different systems function differently and all are upgraded and changed frequently, so it is difficult to discuss specifics. However, it is probably safe to assume that the document will retain the major structural features of the original document, meaning that any properly implemented accessibility features of the original—such as headers and Alt Text tags—for images will result in a Web page

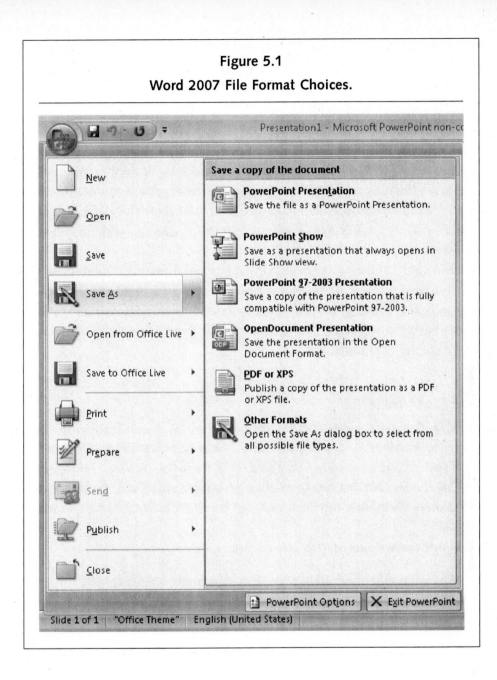

Figure 5.1
Word 2007 File Format Choices.

with those features. (Checking the accessibility of Web pages is covered at the end of the chapter.)

Text Formats: .rtf and .txt

Although many word processors will read documents in .doc or .docx formats, some may not. Rich text format (.rtf), however, retains most of the document features created in Word. It will probably be readable by all word processors and interfaces effectively with assistive technology. Assuming that your document was created following the accessibility tips provided in Chapter Three, the document that the student receives should be equally useful to anyone—with or without a disability.

Plain text (.txt) format strips out all graphics and formatting, keeping just the unadulterated text—no extra space between lines or paragraphs and no formatting to identify headings—which is pretty hard to read. Unless you have a need to provide plain vanilla text to a designer or Web developer, you probably won't have a use for this format.

PDF DOCUMENTS

Portable document format (PDF) was developed by Adobe Systems to allow people to exchange documents that reliably retained their original formatting from one computer to another, independent of the users' software. Almost everyone has the free Acrobat Reader application on their computer these days, and distributing documents in PDF format has become standard practice for many people.

Several methods are used to create PDFs:

- From within the application where the document has been created
- Through Adobe Acrobat or a similar program designed for this and related tasks
- By scanning a hard copy and saving the image as a PDF file

In fact, the first two of these options are the same; although the steps are slightly different, the result is the same, so I will discuss them together. The output of the scanning option is entirely different and is therefore discussed separately.

Creating a PDF from an Electronic Document

PDFs may be a good option for delivering your course materials, since they keep the formatting you intended (as a native format file sometimes will not). Adobe Acrobat, in particular, will permit you to create complex, sophisticated, and accessible PDF documents. Other, free or low-cost PDF-makers available on the Web typically do not provide the same help with ensuring accessibility. However, discussing in depth how to use Acrobat is beyond the scope of this book, as our focus here is on creating content using applications with which you are already familiar.

Microsoft offers a free add-in for Office 2007 that enables you to create PDFs from within those applications. Once installed, it adds the PDF file type to the format list in the Save As dialog box. It cannot output the rich PDF features that Acrobat provides, but it will make a simple PDF document and retain the headers from Word that are so important in creating a document for users of assistive technologies. Another add-in for Word is the PDF Accessibility Wizard (PAW) by Netcentric Technologies which will check the PDF for accessibility and walk authors, step-by-step, through the process to make the necessary corrections in the Word document.

Frequently, authors select PDF as a document format when they want to "lock" the document and prevent the content from being copied. If you do this, it is important that you check the item that makes it accessible to screen reader software. Otherwise, a person who is blind will not be able to read the document.

For anyone wanting to learn how to design accessible PDF documents in Acrobat, I recommend these resources:

- The Adobe Web site has a wide range of information on Acrobat and Flash accessibility at www.adobe.com/accessibility/index.html. This site also has information on how to create accessible Flash content.

- The book *Accessible and Usable PDF Documents: Techniques for Document Authors,* by Karen McCall, is dedicated specifically to creating accessible PDF documents with Acrobat. It is available online at www.karlencommunications .com/products.htm.

- That same Web site has an extensive list of articles related to the topic of PDF accessibility at www.karlencommunications.com/AccessiblePDF.html.

Scanning a Hard-Copy Document to a PDF

Instructors often have a hard-copy document that they would like to share with the class. In a classroom course, they would simply have it copied and hand it out. In an online setting, they will probably scan that document into an electronic format—usually a PDF. However, scanning a document creates a *picture* of the document, not a text document. So a screen reader user accessing this PDF document will be unable to read it.

There is a solution, however. The scanning software should also provide the ability to run optical character recognition (OCR) on the file. This is an important second step in scanning hard copy to a PDF document. When OCR is run, the PDF will include both the picture of the document and the software's best "guess" at the text it represented. Note that this won't be perfect—formatting probably won't be faithfully maintained, page numbers and running heads may be inserted in text, and other errors can appear. But the screen reader software will be able to speak the document's contents. The OCR version has other uses as well. It can be searched by a Web search engine and the text can be manipulated in a word processor. Some scanner software will even send the document directly to a word processor so that it can be distributed in that format.

Converting a Word Document to a Web Page

Both Word 2003 and 2007 let you save a Word document as a Web page using any of three options:

- Single File Web Page (*.mht; *.mhtml)
- Web Page (*.htm; *.html)
- Web Page, Filtered (*.htm; *.html)

Web designers have long complained about the HTML code that Word produces, particularly that in the Single File Web Page and the Web Page formats. So, although it is still less than ideal, the third option, Web Page, Filtered, is the best of the three for repurposing a Word document for the Web—although you may want to run it through a true Web authoring program. (For instance, Adobe Dreamweaver includes a feature for cleaning up Word HTML code.)

You can upload the HTML output from Word to a Web site or to an LMS. If your Word document includes headings and Alt Text tags, and it is correctly uploaded to the system or identified as HTML, your accessibility features should continue to be part of it.

Alternatively, a handy tool for use with Office products is available at www.virtual508.com. The Accessible Wizard walks you step by step through adding Web accessibility features to any Office document. I discuss this wizard in more detail later in the chapter.

Embossed Hard-Copy Braille

Given the accessibility inherently offered by electronic media, you may never need to provide hard-copy Braille content for an online course, and, if it is needed, student disability services will undoubtedly actually create it. Its staff will need to be aware of this process. In case it comes up, here is a brief rundown of the process.

Producing Braille from a Word document is similar to printing a document, except that it requires special software to accomplish a number of special formatting issues and a Braille embosser to output the actual pages. Student disability services will already be providing alternative media, books, handouts, and other content for students on campus. This would be the obvious place for you to look for support if you have a student who requests Braille documents. Most schools and universities will have one or more Braille embossers on campus.

The need for Braille documents is most likely to arise in the context of a math or science course, although these requests are becoming less common as better digital tools for math instruction evolve.

DAISY Format

DAISY—Digital Accessible Information System—is a standard for digital talking books designed primarily to provide a more level reading opportunity for the formerly print disabled population. It offers superior navigation and document control, and as a result, it is being adopted around the world as the answer for students with print disabilities. Many of its concepts are also being integrated into reading tools for people with no apparent disability.

Congress recently mandated that publishers of K–12 textbooks must make them available in an electronic format and specified that the National Instructional Materials Accessibility Standard (NIMAS) format be used. NIMAS is a stripped-down version of DAISY.

Although colleges are currently moving slowly to provide alternate texts in the DAISY format, students in the K–12 grades are increasingly being introduced to this format. When these students reach college, they will expect materials to be available in this format. Thus, although you, as a faculty member, are not likely to have to produce content in DAISY format, you need to know what it is. Staff working in student disability services should definitely be learning about it now, and they may be required to output DAISY content for students with print disabilities.

DAISY documents can be text only, audio only, or text and audio together. The audio can be created by a human reading the text or by a text-to-speech program using a synthetic voice. If there is both text and audio, they can be synchronized so that the word being spoken is the one being displayed and the displayed word can be highlighted. This dual sensory input can be very useful for students with learning and cognitive disabilities.

There is a free add-in for Word that adds a menu item to let you save documents in DAISY format. Because DAISY documents are designed to enhance document navigation, it is important that your Word document be well structured, including the proper use of different headers (see Chapter Three).

DISTRIBUTING EXCEL SPREADSHEETS

The native .xls or .xlsx file format (that is, the actual spreadsheet) is what will best support accessibility for students with disabilities. An Excel spreadsheet can be saved as a Web page, and it will be displayed by assistive technologies including a screen reader, but some information gets lost in the translation. Screen reader users will not be able to navigate the rows and columns with the same degree of understanding as in Excel itself. Students with nonvisual disabilities may handle the Web version as well as they do the Excel version, but a screen reader user could struggle to understand the content—and may even fail.

DISTRIBUTING ACCESSIBLE POWERPOINT CONTENT

Like Word documents, PowerPoint presentations can be saved and distributed in a number of different formats, including native file types (.ppt and .pptx), a

Word document, .rtf, PDF, a Web page, or in hard copy. However, by far the most common choices for online distribution will be sharing either the original PowerPoint presentation or a Web version.

Native PowerPoint Formats

The basic PowerPoint 2003 (.ppt) or 2007 (.pptx) presentation can be uploaded to a learning management system for students to download to their computers. When the presentation has been designed to be accessible, students with disabilities should be able to use these presentations as well as anyone else.

Narrated presentations (.pps and .ptx) can also be uploaded to an LMS and downloaded by the students. As discussed in Chapter Four, if the slide show is designed such that the student can control the navigation, that will be a better study tool than a show that plays automatically.

Exporting PowerPoint Presentations to Word

As mentioned in Chapter Four, PowerPoint slide shows with narration pose problems for students with hearing impairments, and a simple solution is to provide these students with Word output that shows slide images alongside the text of the narration. To do this, a transcript of the narration needs to have been entered in the notes field of each slide. To create a Word version of your PowerPoint presentation, instead of saving it as a .doc file, you need to "publish" it:

- In PowerPoint 2007, from the Office button, go to Publish and then select the Create Handouts in Microsoft Word option.

- There are several formatting options, as shown in Figure 5.2. Some create handouts that provide spaces alongside the slide images for the audience to make notes. Others let you select the arrangement for the slide pictures and speaker notes. Or you can save just the presentation outline as a Word document. Unless the speaker notes are identical to the text in the slide images, only the last choice will provide the slide text for a screen reader user.

PDF Format

If you have Acrobat on your computer, or if you installed the Office save-as-PDF add-in described earlier, the choices for saving file types will include PDF as an

Figure 5.2

Publishing Options for PowerPoint Presentations.

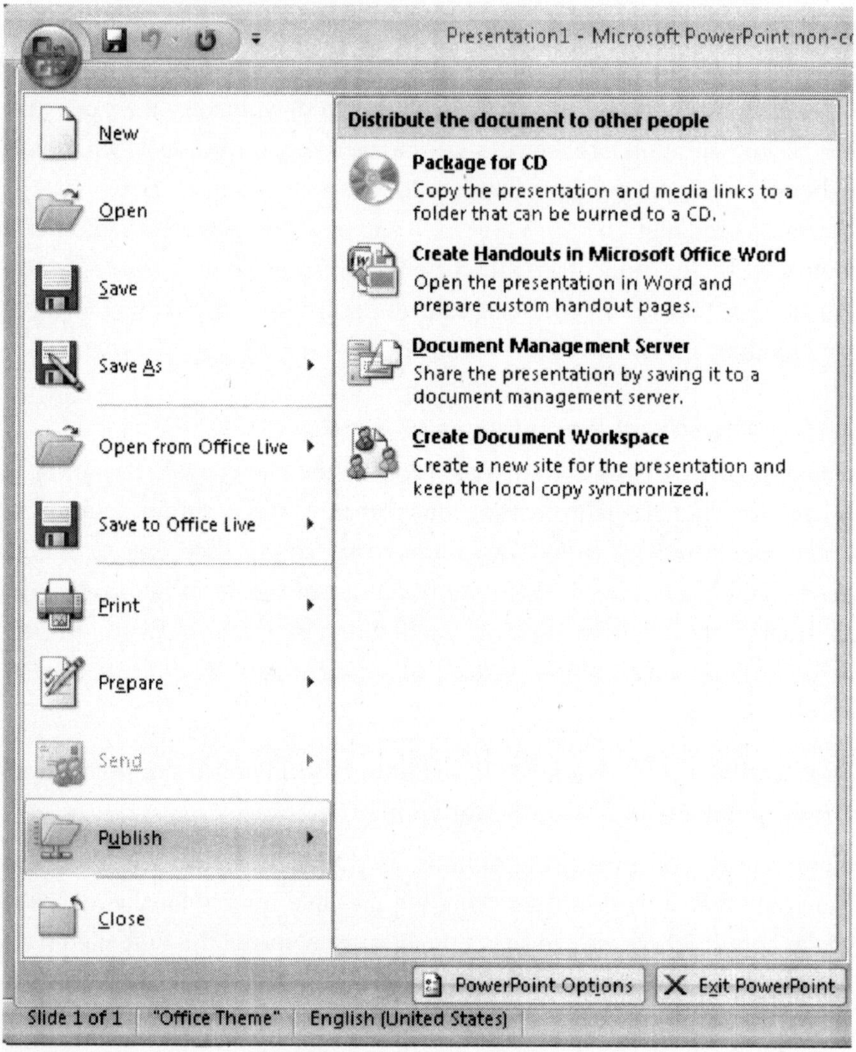

option. PDFs should be accessible to students with disabilities, including those using a screen reader.

Web Pages

The PowerPoint option for outputting presentations in a HTML format results in a set of Web pages with frames and complex navigation. This may be confusing to many users and will probably be difficult for most students with disabilities—although technically it would be accessible to them. I recommend avoiding it.

If, instead, you upload the presentation to your institution's LMS and have it converted to a Web page through the usual process, you should have someone from student disability services look at it for its accessibility. You can also check its accessibility yourself by using one of the toolbar accessibility checkers discussed below. Different learning management systems for repurposing it to Web pages may or may not meet accessibility standards.

Using a utility called LecShare is one of the few ways you can be totally certain that the Web pages will conform to the accessibility standards. LecShare Pro turns a PowerPoint presentation into a series of fully accessible Web pages. It can also be used to add audio to the pages, or it can turn the PowerPoint, with or without accompanying audio, into a video.

You can purchase individual or institutional licenses from the LecShare Web site (www.lecshare.com) for either Mac or PC, and download a fully functioning program. A trial version is also available (it adds a watermark to each slide). LecShare, the "light" version of LecShare Pro, omits the audio functionality.

To create Web pages, you first open LecShare and then import the PowerPoint presentation. Next, the program examines the presentation to identify any accessibility issues. A "slide tray" opens showing the slides, as shown in Figure 5.3. Each slide is identified either as accessible or with the features needing repair highlighted. LecShare then provides options for making the necessary corrections, as Figure 5.4 shows.

When the repairs have been made, you export the presentation in either a Web or video format.

LecShare stores the HTML files that are created in a separate directory. These files can be uploaded to a learning management system or to a Web site; you just need to provide a link from an existing page to the index.htm file that is the

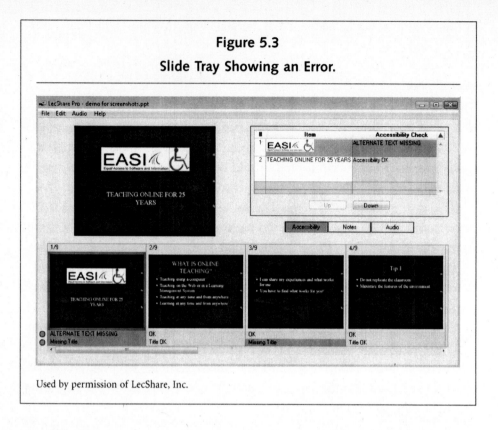

Figure 5.3

Slide Tray Showing an Error.

Used by permission of LecShare, Inc.

beginning of the Web version of the PowerPoint presentation so that students can access it.

As mentioned, you can also use LecShare Pro to record audio for each slide, and the resulting slide show can likewise be turned into a video or a sequence of Web pages. When an audio has been added this way, instead of it playing at each page automatically, each slide has an audio button that the viewer can either use or ignore.

Accessible Wizard for Office

As mentioned earlier, the Accessible Wizard is an add-in product designed to ensure the accessibility of Web pages created from all Office products. It is available in two versions: one for Office 2007 and the other for earlier Office versions, back to 2000. Licenses can be purchased online at www.virtual508.com, and a free limited-use trial is also available (Office 2007 version only).

Figure 5.4

Text Entry Field for Adding a Missing Image Description.

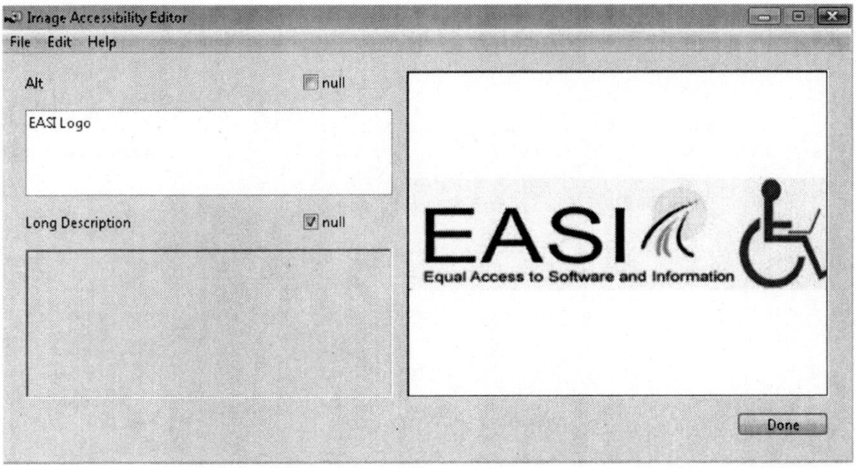

Used by permission of LecShare, Inc.

Once the wizard is installed, it adds new items to the menus of Word and PowerPoint. You can use its capabilities to examine your documents for any accessibility problems. If it locates any, it points to the problem and offers a simple way to fix them. For example, if it locates an image that lacks Alt Text, it shows where the omission occurs and provides a way to fix the problem, as shown in Figure 5.5.

ONLINE ACCESSIBILITY CHECKERS

This chapter has dealt with distributing content, especially distributing it in an online setting. But say you aren't entirely certain about the accessibility of what you have actually posted to your online course. You've done what you're supposed to do, to the best of your understanding to promote accessibility—but do you know if it worked? Fortunately, free tools are available on the Internet that check your pages for accessibility. The two online accessibility checkers I recommend are:

Figure 5.5

The Accessible Wizard's Field for Fixing Errors.

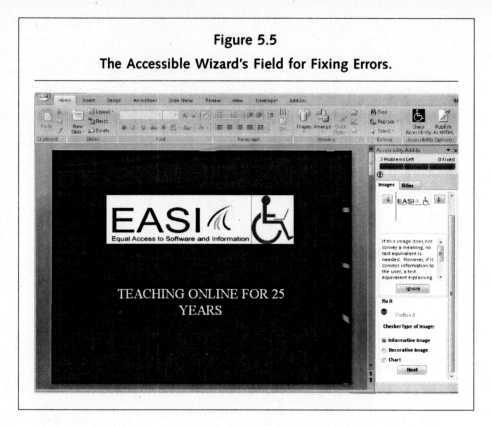

- WAVE, shown in Figure 5.6. part of Utah State University's WebAIM project; available at http://wave.webaim.org.
- Achecker, shown in Figure 5.7, developed by the Assistive Technology Resource Center at the University of Toronto; available at http://achecker.ca/checker/index.php.

To check a Web page with either of these free tools, you access them on the Web and just enter the URL of the page you want to check in the box provided. You will receive a report in return. Alternatively, both tools also will permit you to paste the relevant page's HTML code into a input field.

One limitation of these tools is that in general they will not work for checking the accessibility of pages inside a learning management system, since the pass-

Figure 5.6

WAVE Checker's Access Page.

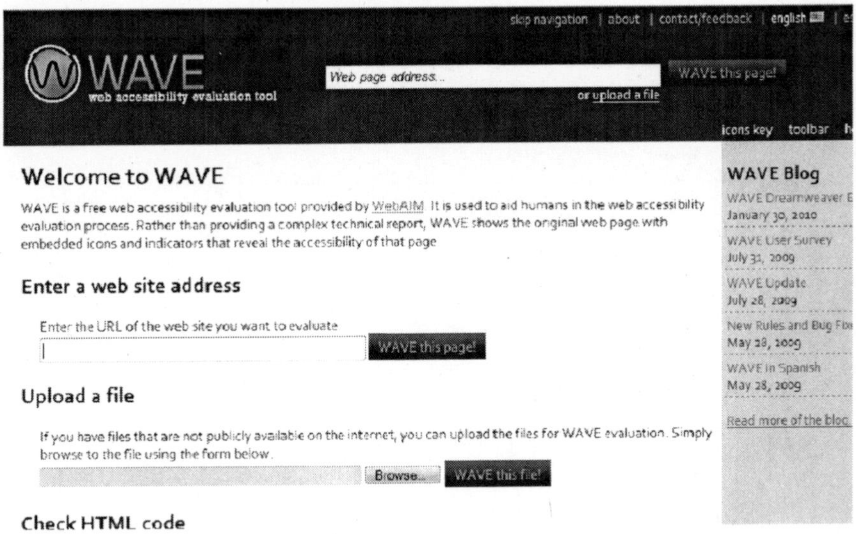

word protection will block their access (although you could still use the paste feature just mentioned). For LMS pages you need a tool you can install inside your browser.

Toolbar Checkers

Two good accessibility toolbars are available for checking the accessibility of password-protected pages. The WAVE toolbar, once installed in the Firefox browser, allows you to check accessibility even inside an LMS. The toolbar is available for free download from http://wave.webaim.org/toolbar.

The Accessible Information Solutions team of Vision Australia provides a similar tool for Internet Explorer; go to http://www.visionaustralia.org.au/ais/toolbar. Although the Web Accessibility Toolbar evaluates pages against version 1.0 of the Web Accessibility Content Guidelines, the features of interest to nontechnical faculty will usually be the same for WCAG versions 1.0 and 2.0.

Figure 5.7

The Achecker Accessibility Evaluation Tool.

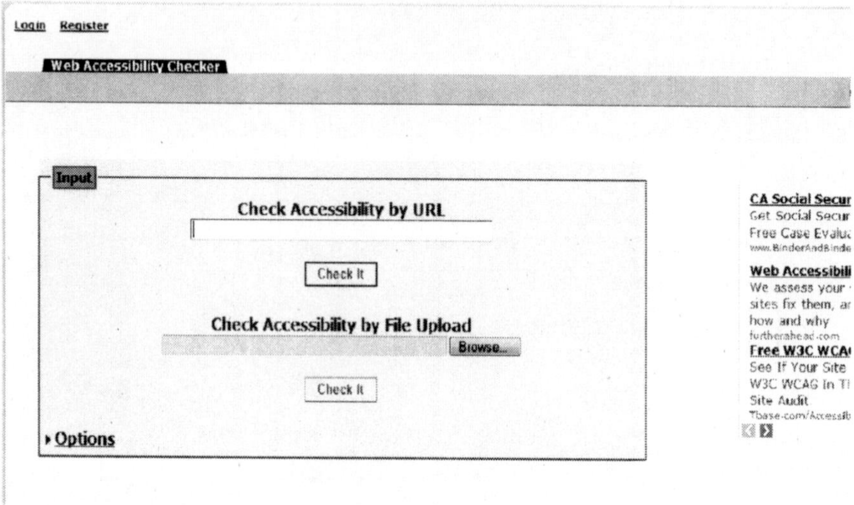

Input

Check Accessibility by URL

Check It

Check Accessibility by File Upload

Browse...

Check It

▸ Options

CA Social Secur
Get Social Secur
Free Case Evalua
www.BinderAndBinde

Web Accessibili
We assess your
sites fix them, ar
how and why
furtherahead.com
Free W3C WCA
See If Your Site
W3C WCAG In Ti
Site Audit
Tbase.com/AccessRi

TAKE-AWAYS FROM THIS CHAPTER

In the previous two chapters, you were introduced to ways to use the power in Microsoft Office applications to create content that will be largely accessible for students with various disabilities. None of it requires much actual extra work. Mainly it requires careful planning and being selective about the features used in the document preparation.

Science, Technology, Engineering, and Math

The disciplines of science, technology, engineering, and math have enough in common that they are frequently lumped together under the acronym STEM. These fields share analogous attitudes toward knowledge and worldviews, and the tools and training they require are also similar. In this chapter I focus on issues of accessibility related to the presentation of math and graphics.

Providing students with disabilities quality access to math and graphics has been historically a daunting challenge. Although students with the specific learning disability known as disnumeria have a processing issue that makes mathematics difficult, it is people who are blind for whom math and graphics have presented the greatest problems in terms of accessibility. The good news is that today's emerging electronic tools enable these students to compete and succeed in STEM fields as never before.

HISTORICAL ISSUES WITH MATH ACCESSIBILITY

In the rest of this book, I minimize the presentation of background information and focus on what a faculty member needs to know today to produce accessible course content. However, in this case, the technology will make more sense if it is viewed in the context of the difficulties faced in the past by people with disabilities attempting to access math and technical content.

Spoken Math

Often people who are blind can rely on hearing to compensate (in part) for their lack of sight. Think of audio books and screen readers. Yet with math, unambiguous oral communication can be very difficult. The following example will highlight how easy it is for a listener to hear something quite different from what the speaker meant.

Imagine you're back in your beginning algebra class, but for some reason the blackboard has been taken away. The teacher gives the class a problem verbally: "A plus B over C equals X." How do you know whether she means this:

$$\frac{A+B}{C} = X$$

or this?

$$A + \frac{B}{C} = X$$

These two equations sound identical but have very different meanings, mathematically. Without seeing the equation or some fuller explanation, you could not know which the teacher meant—this is the situation faced by someone who is blind and who obtains math information by someone reading it.

Written Math

Literary Braille is entirely unsuited to rendering math. The slate and stylus used to write Braille have severe limitations when it comes to writing and solving math problems. As a result, in math courses taught at schools for the blind, instead of teaching math using Braille, the teachers used other devices. The Taylor slate, which was designed for students to do arithmetic, consisted of a matrix of holes and a number of cubes with raised symbols on them which could be inserted into those holes. It was totally inadequate for doing higher math (Kubiak-Becker and Dick, 1996).

Another limitation of literary Braille in representing math was that it uses a six-dot matrix, so the total number of possible symbols is restricted to A–Z, 0–9, and a few symbols for punctuation and capitalization—hardly adequate for advanced math. In addition, standard Braille is intended to reproduce horizontal linear text, like that you are reading right now. But math includes a vertical component as well: placement above or below the baseline is vital to convey its meaning.

In a video produced by the DO-IT Project at the University of Washington, a professor confessed that he had thought it impossible to do advanced math without seeing it. Not unusually, for him, math included a significant visual component (DO-IT Video, 1994). Yet there are prominent blind mathematicians and scientists. Abraham Nemeth, blind from birth, earned a PhD in math from Columbia and Wayne State Universities and taught for thirty years at the University of Detroit Mercy. He devised a system whereby someone could read an equation to him without introducing verbal ambiguities (more on this shortly), and he built on that to design a special Braille math code that could clearly render math by overcoming the problems mentioned above (Nemeth, 1996). His code reassigned some of the standard literary Braille symbols so that they would represent math symbols.

In time, Nemeth's written system became recognized by the Braille Authority of North America as the standard way to represent advanced math. The *Nemeth Braille Code for Mathematics* was published by the American Printing House for the Blind in 1952 and has been updated several times over the years since. However, Nemeth's system could not completely overcome the limitations of Braille's linearity. A Braille symbol can indicate that an item should be *thought of* as being above or below the line, but it is left to the reader to imagine that placement rather than being able to actually perceive it. Solving this problem had to wait for the digital revolution.

AUTHORING ACCESSIBLE ELECTRONIC MATH DOCUMENTS

Two important events in the 1990s prepared the way to change the serious barriers to math and science for students with disabilities. The National Science Foundation (NSF) officially established the Program for Persons with Disabilities (PPD) late in 1991, appointing Dr. Larry Scadden its senior program director early in 1992 (Scadden, 2008). The program funded over one hundred projects while he was the program officer, many of which supported university programs that provided extensive support for students with disabilities, including raising teacher awareness, providing teachers with tips to help them meet student needs, and often including significant peer mentoring. An important, but smaller, number supported research projects aimed at producing new technologies.

The second event was a symposium in 1994 on math and science hosted by Recording for the Blind and Dyslexic (RFB&D) to which over three dozen experts were invited from around the world. The symposium's goal was to transform the tools available to people with disabilities for accessing math and science (Jones, 1994).

The participants included researchers, teachers, publishers, and other interested individuals. By the end of the event, consensus had been reached that computer applications needed to be developed that could take existing math representations and present them in such a way that people with disabilities could understand. Specifically, the computer representation of advanced math needed to be improved, as well as the assistive computer applications used by students with disabilities, so that their special assistive software could better understand math and technical content. The NSF creation of the Program for Persons with Disabilities combined with the RFB&D symposium together jump-started projects across the country, thus resulting in significant progress in these fields.

The basic ASCII code that early personal computers used to represent letters and numbers, like Braille, lacked a way to represent many of the symbols common in advanced math. Math formulas frequently used graphics to represent some advanced formulae when their symbols were not included in the ASCII code. Some attempts at providing accessibility for a blind computer reader tried embedding an audio in that graphic explaining it, but the symposium members strongly pointed out the inadequacy of this solution.

Eventually, this deficit was resolved by the creation of MathML, an international standard markup language for representing math. Although it is a significant advance in Web pages' ability to display and manipulate math expressions, the markup features also make it possible for screen readers and other assistive technologies to interface with the math. MathML, however, solves only half of the problems of providing access to math in electronic format for screen reader users who are blind. The screen reader software still has to verbalize the math in a meaningful and dependable manner. That's where Nemeth's system for spoken math comes in.

Protocol for Spoken Math: MathSpeak

As mentioned earlier, before he devised a way to express advanced math in Braille, Abraham Nemeth had developed a personal set of rules for spoken math

(Nemeth, 1995), as he depended on human readers. David Schleppenbach contracted with Nemeth to develop a formal spoken math protocol for his company gh, LLC, which is devoted to providing math and scientific documents for people who are blind. (gh LLC provides documents in Nemeth Braille and it has developed the gh PLAYER™ for DAISY Books, NIMAS files, and other e-book formats.)

Let's return to the simple but ambiguous math expressions we saw before, and see how they would be treated by MathSpeak. The first equation,

$$\frac{A+B}{C} = X$$

would be read "(start frac) A plus B over C (end frac) equals X," whereas

$$A + \frac{B}{C} = X$$

would be "A plus (start frac) B over C (end frac) equals X."

The protocol for MathSpeak for anyone who would like to see the entire system is available online at http://www.gh-mathspeak.com.

Primarily, however, this discussion has been a preamble for a description of two complementary tools that are essential to faculty who need to provide accessible math content and students who are blind and need to access that content: MathType and MathPlayer. Staff from student disability services, if they are not already aware of this, will want to know about MathPlayer so they can better support math students with disabilities.

MathType and MathPlayer

By now you have some understanding of the obstacles and steps in the quest to provide accessible math for students with disabilities. The good news is that that goal has, at last, been achieved. Providing accessible math for the Web is now simple and almost painless for content authors. Design Science Inc. has developed a number of useful tools related to math and science. Microsoft licensed its Equation Editor, and it is the standard math editor for Word.

Design Science's MathType is an advanced version of Equation Editor, and one of its features is that it provides the output in an accessible format. MathType can be used either as a stand-alone application or as an add-in for Word. The latter adds another tab to Word's main ribbon. To output accessible content:

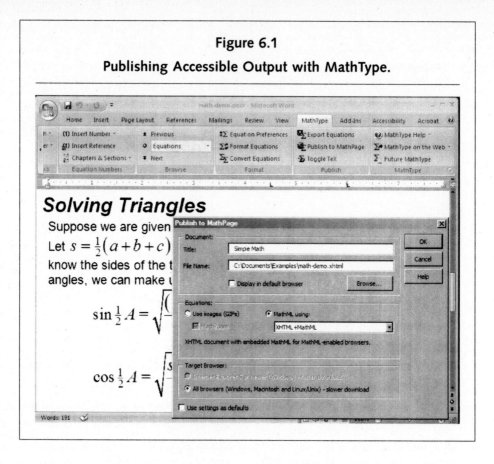

Figure 6.1

Publishing Accessible Output with MathType.

1. Start by simply inputting math in Word as you normally would. You don't have to think about accessibility issues until you're done.

2. At that point, instead of using the Save option, use the Publish to MathPage option on the MathType tab, and enter a file name as shown in Figure 6.1.

3. To provide a Web page containing math that is accessible for students using a screen reader, choose to have the equations displayed in MathML format, not as images as shown in Figure 6.2. The file type should be either .xhtml or .xht.

4. Be sure to select that it will display in Internet Explorer or in all browsers.

Note: MathType also works with the other Office programs and a large number of proprietary, open source, and online applications. See the Design

Figure 6.2

Displaying Equations in MathML Format.

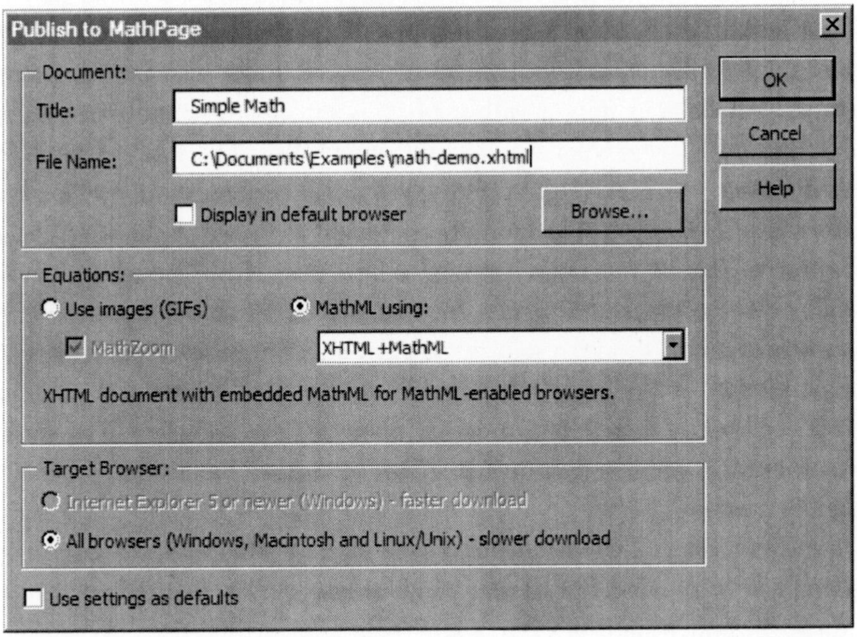

Science site: www.dessci.com. Students using screen reader software will need the free MathPlayer, which is an extension to Internet Explorer version 6 or above. The student hears the math read aloud in MathSpeak, giving them access to the content comparable to that of other students. These two applications, MathType and MathPlayer, have revolutionized online math learning for students who are blind.

ISSUES WITH TECHNICAL GRAPHICS

While math content will sometimes include diagrams, science, technology, and engineering courses often rely heavily on graphical representations to make their content understandable. Because our focus is on courses delivered online, this section is primarily concerned with Web graphics.

Obviously, students with upper body motor impairments and those with hearing impairments will have no more difficulty understanding a graphic on the Web than would a student who has no disability. Students with learning disabilities should have few if any problems with online graphics, and in fact they frequently benefit from visual representations of information. Graphics on Web pages can be problematic for students with limited vision who are using screen magnification software, but as with math, it is students who are blind and rely on a screen reader who will have the most serious difficulties with graphics.

As discussed in earlier chapters, although a screen reader cannot itself describe an image, the Web page can include alternative text for it, which the screen reader will vocalize. The Alt Text tag is intended to be a short label. The author can also include a link to a longer description, but that still may be an inadequate solution. There are situations in which information can only be conveyed adequately in a graphic format. For example, when the relationships of interrelated parts of a system are what is most relevant, words alone are not sufficient. The student needs to experience these relationships either by sight or by touch to thoroughly grasp the meaning.

In the past, many different methods were used to provide tactile graphics for students who were blind, but all were cumbersome and less than satisfactory. For example, pins might be stuck into a cork board and strings used to "draw" the lines between these points (Kubiak-Becker & Dick, 1996). Another method is to use "swell paper" to produce raised line drawings. The image would be drawn on the paper in black ink, and then the paper was subjected to heat which created a raised line where the ink was (Gardner, 1996). These methods were time-consuming and could not fill the day-to-day needs of a class making extensive use of graphics.

PROVIDING ACCESSIBLE GRAPHICS

Fortunately, new technologies offer better and less-expensive options for producing tactile graphics. Unfortunately for those delivering (and taking) courses online, hard-copy tactile graphics are as yet the only true solution. There is currently no technical way to provide true online accessibility. So these graphics need to be produced to order and delivered to the student in person or by "snail mail" in time for the corresponding online lesson.

The Instructor's Role

The embossing equipment (see below) and the software needed to produce tactile graphics is rather expensive, and the process is less than automatic. Someone has to repurpose the online graphic—usually the Student Disability Services office or equivalent department. However, that does not mean the instructor won't need to be involved. The graphic will require some modification because although the eye can readily understand graphics with a fine resolution, fingers are less sensitive, so the graphic will need to be scaled up.

Sometimes, merely providing a larger graphic is adequate. Other times, to make the details discernable to touch, the enlargement will need to be larger than the largest paper the embosser can handle. In this case someone will have to think about how to modify the graphic and keep its meaning. For example, you might need several graphics: one providing an overview and several "tiles" showing portions of the original. Only the teacher will be able to oversee such a modification and know it still conveys the desired meaning.

The other way that the teacher should be involved is in providing some direction to the student using the graphic about how to interpret or understand it, because someone examining an object by touch will approach the task differently from someone who can see it. The sighted person would take in the object as a whole, and only then begin to look at its parts and their relationships. People who are blind and exploring by touch experience the parts of the object first, and then mentally combine them to construct an image of the whole (Mack, 1993). The instructor can help the tactile graphic's users by providing written direction about the overall structure and where best to start examining the graphic. Again, the teacher rather than the person who creates the tactile version needs to do this task.

Note: It is always a good practice for online faculty who may need the assistance of student disability services to develop a personal connection with staff in that office. Due to the various accessibility issues and the collaborative nature of providing tactile graphics, those teaching math and science courses will benefit more than most from this interdepartmental cooperation.

How Braille Embossers Work

Although handling the actual equipment will normally be done by student disability services, let's look briefly at what is involved.

There are a number of different Braille embossers on the market. Almost all are primarily designed to produce standard Braille rather than tactile graphics. If you've ever seen a page of Braille, you might think that the dots used to form the characters could easily be used instead to make images. However, traditional Braille embossers work like an old dot matrix printer: they mainly just produce dots in the six-dot Braille matrix and lack the flexibility to make anything more complex.

ViewPlus Technologies has developed a line of embossers that can also emboss dots in almost any imaginable arrangement—making graphics composed of embossed dots possible. (They also print standard literary or Nemeth Braille.) In addition to arranging dots in any order, these machines can also create dots of different heights and place them densely or sparsely, as needed, to improve the three-dimensionality of representations. Another ViewPlus printer, Emprint SpotDot, simultaneously prints Braille, tactile graphics, and inkjet text and images, thus simplifying the task of providing materials in different modalities.

TAKE-AWAYS FROM THIS CHAPTER

This chapter has focused on what teachers can do to support students with disabilities. To create online math content that is accessible for all students, including those with disabilities, the teacher should

- Install MathType.
- Publish the document as MathML (file extension of .xhtml or .xht).
- Upload the file to the Web or to a learning management system as a Web page.

Tactile graphics for students with significant visual impairments (and perhaps learning disabilities) cannot be made accessible in the online setting and will necessitate the production of hard copy to be delivered outside of the online context. Although student disability services will do the actual production, faculty will want to remain involved to be sure the tactile graphic is still true to what was intended. The teacher should also provide students with some information to help make sense of the tactile representation.

The advances made in the accessibility of math and graphics that have occurred over the last two decades are exciting. Although for a long time progress toward accessibility has been painfully slow, students with disabilities can now compete successfully in the STEM disciplines.

Besides the technical advances touched on in this chapter, a number of innovative projects are being conducted at universities around the globe. A group of researchers in Japan developed a package of software tools to help in authoring accessible math and to make math accessible to a reader who is blind (Suzuki and Yamaguchi, 2008). New and even more powerful tools will result from this global research, and faculty and staff should be ready to adopt them when they become available.

Making Multimedia Accessible

The term *multimedia* covers a variety of applications and technologies, which are used in numerous ways for various purposes. It implies the simultaneous use of more than one medium such as audio, text, visuals including images, and video. Each of the types of disabilities discussed in the book so far can be affected by these applications in different ways. In this chapter I describe the advantages multimedia can provide and the accessibility problems it can pose for students with different disabilities, including

- How multimedia can support the learning of students with disabilities
- The problems multimedia can pose for these students
- How to increase accessibility with synchronized captions

Clearly, creating multimedia content is a complex topic that far exceeds what this book sets out to accomplish. Instead, I concentrate on simple tools and strategies related to accessibility that can be used by almost anyone, not just those who want to become multimedia experts.

THE ROLE OF MULTIMEDIA IN ONLINE LEARNING

Multimedia can be seductive for those of us who love technology—so much so that we might be tempted to use it for its own sake. In an article entitled

"Multimedia and Learning," usability expert Bob Bailey states categorically that "there is no question that multimedia, used appropriately, can improve a person's ability to learn and remember the contents of a Web site" (Bailey, 2001). In the same article, however, Bailey warns about inappropriate uses of multimedia, which echoes a point I made in earlier chapters that in communication every element should contribute to the point of the discussion. Irrelevant media can distract learners and actually decrease student learning.

In an excellent article on the same subject, instructional designer Patti Shank says that effective use of multimedia requires combining media in ways that take advantage of each medium's unique characteristics, but adds the caveat that because multimedia requires the use of multiple senses, "you must consider the implications of each medium on people who have visual, auditory, or other disabilities" (Shank, 2005).

Effective Uses of Multimedia

Frequently, authors mistakenly assume that an object they include in a document—whether a picture, chart, audio track, or embedded video file—will speak for itself. They know what it means, after all, but they may overlook the necessity to provide less-initiated readers (or students) with the context that will help them understand that meaning. In short, to use multimedia effectively, you need to tell the reader what it is meant to convey.

Bailey (2001) provides the following guidelines for using multimedia more effectively:

- Use text to reinforce an image or video (including text captions and labels). This will enhance its accessibility for those with visual or hearing impairments.

- Reveal information systematically, not all at once. For example, entertainment multimedia is often awash in sounds and images that are intended to heighten the viewer's experience. But to people with an attention deficit or other disability, this barrage of information can be very distracting.

- Avoid animation or displaying motion simultaneously with other content, as the animation will draw attention away from the other content.

Bailey (2001) also contends that when a teacher is using multimedia, the content presented in one medium needs to support and extend the information presented in the other medium. In this he is in agreement with the National Center on Universal Design for Learning's guideline (2010) about providing multiple ways for learners to engage and interact with content, as discussed in Chapter One. The use of closely related, supportive graphics that supplement verbal information (text or audio) improves learning. Multimedia can also be used effectively to direct the learner's focus to the most relevant information on a page. The bottom line is that when graphics, video, audio, or other media can enhance and support content, they are appropriate and will strengthen the lesson for students—with or without disabilities. Otherwise, they are best omitted.

Issues with Multimedia for Students with Disabilities

Multimedia that has audio and video components frequently has at least one of the following accessibility issues. These require that additional information be incorporated to ensure the media are accessible to people with certain disabilities:

- Spoken content will have to be provided as text for people with hearing impairments. This text is usually referred to as a *transcription* when it is not synchronized or as *captioning* when it is synchronized.

- Any important silent action in a video will require an alternative means of conveying that action to someone with a visual impairment. This is generally called *descriptive video* and is usually additional spoken audio that describes the action.

As mentioned previously, multimedia has both benefits and deficits for people with disabilities. On the one hand, due to multimedia's use of multiple senses, some elements will be totally inaccessible to people with a specific disability. On the other hand, the use of redundant multimedia modes makes it possible to reach all disability groups—provided the multimedia was designed to do that.

The disability group that has the fewest difficulties with multimedia content is people with motor impairments. They may, however, have problems with the controls in the player used to display the multimedia, as sometimes the mouse is necessary to start, pause, stop, or change the volume. Those with motor impairments who rely on the keyboard or an application such as voice recognition that replicates the keyboard will not be able to use these controls. In other respects, these people's experience of the multimedia will be similar to that of people with no disability.

As noted above, when multimedia provides *different* information simultaneously in two modes, people with learning disabilities can easily become confused and distracted. If, instead, the multimedia presents the *same* content simultaneously in two modes, it will help this person maintain attention and focus. The redundant communication will support the learning of a person with a learning disability more than information presented only in a single sensory mode.

People with visual impairments, especially those who are blind, will miss any content that is presented only in a visual mode. Similarly, people with hearing impairments will totally miss any information provided exclusively in an audio form.

A Word about Flash

Adobe Flash has become popular with many designers, and many multimedia authoring tools, including Camtasia, which I discuss in this chapter, allow you to save their output in Flash-compatible formats. In the past, Flash had a number of accessibility problems; for example, the Flash Player audio/video controls were inaccessible from the keyboard. That is no longer true. Adobe has been working to resolve these issues and continues to work to build in features that will make it interact better with assistive technologies. However, for the time being full accessibility is still far from automatic, so it is probably better not to design your multimedia in Flash. If you are using a commercial multimedia authoring tool that uses the Flash player for one of its output choices, it will be accessible now that the Flash player is keyboard accessible. Information on making Flash output that is accessible for people with disabilities is available from Adobe at www.adobe.com/accessibility/products/flash/.

Social Media

Social media such as Facebook and Twitter change their interface so frequently that making statements about their accessibility is difficult. Parts of these sites are heavily visual and also filled with dense features making for accessibility problems. Other parts that focus more on reading and leaving messages are more likely to be accessible. Many people with disabilities use these popular sites in spite of the problems. If a teacher integrates their use in a course, their limitations should be kept in mind. The faculty could ask the staff of student disability services to evaluate whether the application that the students would need could be a learning barrier or not. If so, the teacher may need to provide that content some other way. People with disabilities using these sites report that the mobile interface is easier to use, as it is a stripped-down version of the site and therefore frequently less confusing. The accessibletwitter.com interface and the m.facebook.com interface are worth trying as well.

CREATING A TRANSCRIPT

As mentioned, spoken audio content requires a transcript for people who have a hearing impairment. (Obviously, an audio of a Bach concerto or a similar musical presentation would not have a transcript.) The audio and the transcript would have separate links on the page they were accessed from. Someone with hearing would listen to the audio while someone who is hearing-impaired would read the text. There is no need to synchronize the audio and transcript in order for the person who is deaf to fully understand the content.

Transcripts of audio content offer several advantages even for students with normal hearing:

- Skimming the text is quicker than listening to the audio.
- The reader can underline and annotate the text.
- The text can more easily be shared with others.
- Listening tends to be a passive activity, whereas reading is more active and therefore better for learning.

Creating a transcript, whether of an audio-only presentation or of the spoken content in a video can be time-consuming and tedious. A transcriber has to listen to the recorded spoken content, pausing it, backing up, and repeatedly listening to it in order to produce an accurate transcript. However, this is still a better option than using voice recognition software. The error rate for the latter is much too high, and correcting the mistakes is even less efficient than transcribing from the recording. When possible, the best way to get an accurate transcription is for the speaker to follow a written script when recording the presentation. The script would then serve as the transcript.

ADDING SYNCHRONIZED CAPTIONS TO A VIDEO

Dozens of both free and commercial multimedia authoring tools are available, and many will also give you the ability to caption any video you create. It is impossible to say which of these applications is best. However, I believe that for a nonexpert the "best" application is to select the one being used by your friends. Most of us need help from time to time, and consulting tech support is usually a frustrating and time-consuming task. Friends are the best support system there is. The following sections describe two popular applications that facilitate synchronizing captions for your video content: MAGpie and Camtasia.

Using MAGpie

The free Media Access Generator, or MAGpie, was developed by the nonprofit National Center for Accessible Media (NCAM) as a tool for enabling multimedia authors to add synchronized captions and video descriptions to streaming videos. (Users with limited technical background may prefer one of the commercial products.) Both the MAGpie software and information on how to use it can be downloaded from the NCAM Web site: http://ncam.wgbh.org. The following is a brief summary of the software's captioning process.

MAGpie creates captions by using several files that are designed to work together:

- The video
- The text file formatted with the line length that MAGpie requires
- The program that MAGpie creates to control the synchronization

After you open MAGpie, you will follow these steps, as depicted in Figure 7.1:

1. Start by importing the video and the transcript, and then click the control to start the video.

2. The caption window shows only the three or four lines that will fit into the standard caption area provided in the player. When the spoken audio content finishes that text, click on the control to advance the text. This creates a time stamp.

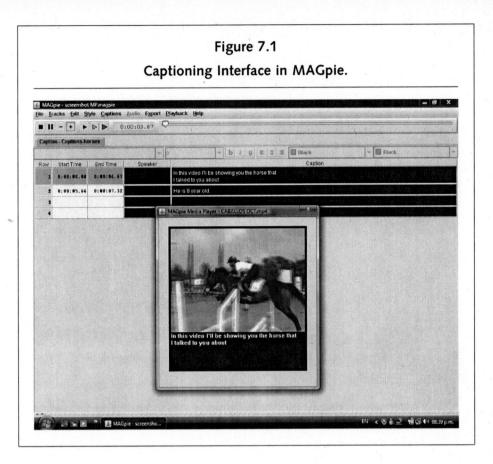

Figure 7.1

Captioning Interface in MAGpie.

3. Repeat step 2 each time the displayed text has been spoken, until you have captioned the entire video.

4. When you are finished, save your work to one of the file types MAGpie supports.

If the presentation is lengthy, this process can become somewhat mind-numbing, and some mistakes are probably inevitable. Fortunately, MAGpie does provide a way to edit and correct timing errors.

Captioning with Camtasia

Camtasia Studio and Camtasia:mac, made by Tech Smith (www.techsmith.com), are some of the most popular multimedia authoring tools on the market, so you probably already have colleagues who use one or the other, depending on their

Figure 7.2

Camtasia's Opening Interface.

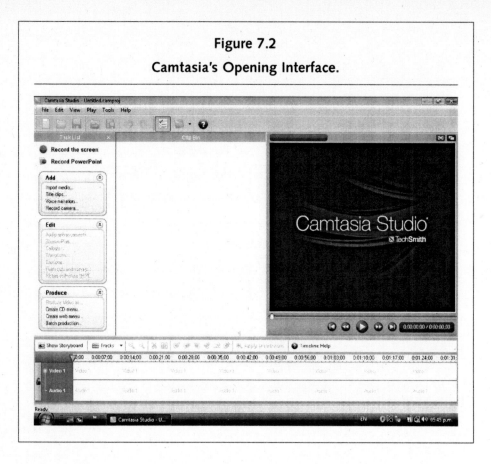

computer platform. Other commercial authoring tools follow an analogous captioning process, so the following description will be pertinent even if you end up choosing different software.

When you open Camtasia, you will find three panels, as shown in Figure 7.2. The Task List panel, on the left, will let you make a recording or record narration for a PowerPoint slide show. You can also access all of your related files here. This panel has three sections: Add, Edit, and Produce. The center panel is the Clip Bin. Every file you have imported, produced, or recorded will be represented there with a thumbnail or icon. The right panel contains the Player, where you can watch the video while inputting the time stamps to synchronize the captions. Across the bottom of the screen is the Timeline, which shows the options that you will use in assembling the parts of your captioned media.

Synchronizing Captions

To add synchronized captions:

1. In the Add panel, navigate to the finished video file you want to caption. When you add the file to the Camtasia project, a thumbnail for it appears in the Clip Bin.

2. Drag the thumbnail to the Timeline, go to the Edit section of the Task List, and click Captions. A new window is then displayed in the left side of your screen, as shown in Figure 7.3.

3. Paste your previously prepared text into this window. Camtasia will format it correctly so that the line length is appropriate for captioning. You can also set the number of characters you want the captions to have; the default is thirty-two characters.

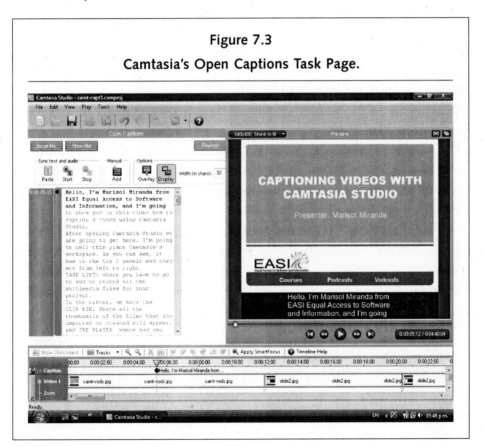

Figure 7.3
Camtasia's Open Captions Task Page.

4. The first caption is inserted the moment that the text is pasted in. Note that the first three lines of the text are in black; this will be the first caption. The rest of the text is red. Click the Start button (located in the captions window) to play the video and begin adding time stamps.

5. Position your cursor on the first word in the transcription text that is in red. When the speaker in the audio reaches that word, click on it. This inserts a new caption point, and the next three lines change to black, as they have become the active caption.

6. Repeat step 5 until you've reached the end of the video and then save your work.

Open or Closed Captions?

Open captioning means that the captions are always visible, with no way for the viewer to turn them off. Conversely, *closed captioning* means that the viewer must click on a button to have the captions become visible.

You can save and deliver your captioned video in several different multimedia formats, as shown in Figure 7.4. If you elect to have Camtasia produce the multimedia to use on the Web, the output will result in an embedded video that will be viewed in Flash Player.

To output the video with captions, Camtasia's Display Captions button must be enabled, as it is by default during the captioning process. The Options button lets you switch between having the captions overlaid on the video or displayed beneath it; you can preview the two effects by clicking the button.

If you select the video to have closed captions, viewers who want to see the captions can use a button on the Flash Player to make them visible. If, however, you select open captions, they will always be displayed in the player. Because the viewer will have no control over them, you might want to provide a second, noncaptioned version of the video for viewers who don't need them.

Including Video Descriptions

Audio descriptions of important actions or other visual elements in a video that are silent require additional audio to be inserted into the video to inform a person who is blind about that important action. Adding this additional audio is rather complex:

Figure 7.4
Camtasia's Output Choices.

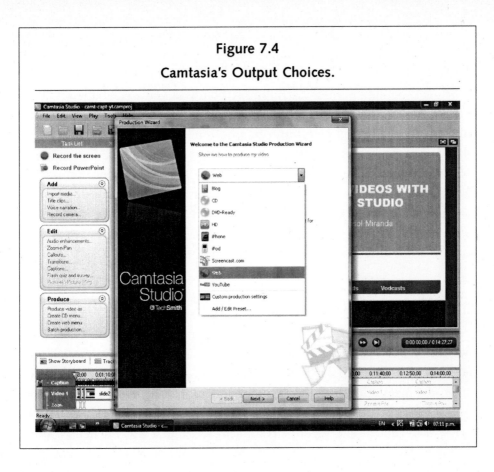

- The description must be composed thoughtfully with an awareness of what a person who is blind will need to know without its becoming lengthy and patronizing.

- The description has to be recorded and synchronized with the video.

- The extra audio must not conflict with the rest of the audio, so it has to be squeezed into existing silent spots in the video—without altering its natural flow.

- Viewers who are not blind and who would find the description annoying must be able to turn it on and off.

Both Camtasia and MAGpie include the ability to produce video description, but the complexity of the process puts it beyond the scope of this book. So, even though a skilled user of today's multimedia applications will probably be able to do the job, I'd like to suggest a simpler solution for faculty creating educational videos.

Before shooting the video, carefully envision what you will be doing. Whenever you will be taking some action important to the content of the lesson, be sure that the dialog will help someone who cannot see the action understand what you are doing and why. If you narrate what you are doing as you go along, video description will most likely be unnecessary. Besides providing information for someone with a visual impairment, you will also be helping anyone who may have become distracted—and let's face it, who doesn't, from time to time? By providing that information in dual sensory modes, you reinforce its importance for your entire audience.

ACCESSIBILITY FOR REAL-TIME AUDIO OR VIDEO

Frequently, you will encounter live streaming audio and video on either the Internet or in a learning management system. Similarly, educators commonly make use of live Web conferences. In such a case, to ensure accessibility, employ one of the many commercial transcribing and captioning services that support real-time events. Different vendors use similar but slightly different systems to take spoken content and input its equivalent text into a window that supports streaming text. As mentioned earlier, voice recognition is not yet capable of accurately transcribing spoken content. Usually the captioner uses the kind of device courtroom stenographers use to input phonetic symbols, not the actual letter-by-letter content, and a computer program changes that data into text and streams it to users on the Internet.

TAKE-AWAYS FROM THIS CHAPTER

Without question, using multimedia does enrich course content. It can provide a refreshing change of pace from all—or mostly—text content. It can add interest and it is excellent at evoking feeling and motivation. Finally, multimedia can sometimes convey the information more clearly than other content formats. Even though it takes more time to create, the value it can bring to a course frequently makes that extra effort worthwhile.

In using multimedia, keep these three principles in mind:

- Keep it simple.
- Keep it short.
- Keep it relevant.

There are two reasons for you to keep your multimedia simple. First, that will help you keep it clear and focused. Second, you will be able to learn to produce it yourself. If you have to depend on others to create it, you may find your project in a long production waiting line.

Perhaps the most important of these three points is the advice to keep the content relevant. Then it will reinforce the point that you are making, and it will add a more persuasive thrust to the lesson.

Supporting Accessible Online Learning

U p to this point in the book, we have been looking primarily at how faculty can ensure the accessibility of their online courses and secondarily at how staff in information technology and student disability services can support that effort. However, without support from above—from administration at the department and institution levels—those efforts will be far more difficult and may largely fail.

THE NEED FOR INSTITUTION-WIDE SUPPORT

In fact, the Department of Education's Office for Civil Rights (OCR) has stated that supporting the needs of students with disabilities is the responsibility of the institution as a whole (U.S. Dept. of Education, 1998). Of course, the danger in assigning the responsibility for supporting online accessibility to the entire institution is that, sometimes, when everyone is responsible, nobody actually takes responsibility. For example, when my college, the Rochester Institute of Technology, recognized it needed to have a Braille embosser, the decision dragged on for over six months without a decision. For some reason, the decision would be made by either the academic computing department, student affairs, or the library, and they could not agree on who would actually pay. I finally located some funds and purchased it with that.

This is why some structure for focusing responsibility needs to be designed. University structures tend to be egalitarian rather than authoritarian; creating an interdepartmental support team will be more effective. But the decision to form such a team gives rise to a new set of questions:

- Who should be on the support team; what departments and offices should be represented?
- How should the team be structured?
- How should people be chosen or recruited to be a part of the team?
- Who does the team support?
- What rules or policies will guide the team in its efforts?

Let's look at each of these questions in turn.

Who Should Be on the Support Team?

The following people and groups should be considered when forming a support team, although in any given team, not all of these parties will necessarily be involved:

- Online learning department staff
- Academic computing staff
- A representative from the faculty governance organization
- One or more online faculty (perhaps one from each different discipline area)
- Instructional design staff
- Multimedia creation staff
- Representative of the students with disabilities
- Student disability services staff
- Alternative text production staff
- Library staff
- Institution Web master or a representative
- ADA compliance officer
- Representative from the office of the provost or president
- Representative from the finance office

How Should the Team Be Structured?

The first question to decide is "how much formal structure should your team have?" In my experience the more formal structure there is, the more issues get framed in a bureaucratic format. When the team is more a discussion among people caring about the same issue, the easier it is to reach consensus. However, if the team is large as suggested here, there may be a benefit from having a smaller steering committee for dealing with day-to-day activities. On the one hand, this steering committee could emerge from those with the most burning passion for accessibility; on the other hand, the steering committee could involve the areas most concerned with online learning: the online learning department, the faculty, and someone from a more technical background.

There is a question as to whether someone from the administration should be on this smaller leadership group too. Personally, I would worry that that might bring a more hierarchical flavor into the committee. I doubt there is a correct answer to this decision.

How Are Team Members Chosen?

How can you best identify which individuals from these areas should be invited to join the team? If you can either get volunteers or approach people who you know have an interest in making online learning more accessible, use this approach. Beware of having a department assign someone, as, in my experience, the individual may be chosen because he or she is at the bottom of the department's hierarchy rather than being someone with an accessibility concern.

Although it is crucial to get visible support from either the provost or president (as discussed later in the chapter), the team should be clearly seen as representing the rank and file of faculty, staff, and students with disabilities. No one likes being dictated to. The team needs to have a broad buy-in from a community committed to providing quality learning opportunities to all students.

Who Does the Team Support?

Being clear on which people and activities are being supported will help the team focus its mission. I believe that the team should support at least the following three groups:

- Students with disabilities taking online courses
- Faculty and instructional design staff creating online content
- Information technology staff responsible for installing and managing the actual learning management system program and for supporting faculty in learning how to use it

Supporting the accessibility needs of students with disabilities taking online courses could, at one time or another, involve several members of the team. Supporting a faculty member or an instructional design staff person creating course content could draw on the skills of people and departments with different specializations. Instead of the content author floundering alone or scrambling to locate someone to provide assistance, the team would provide a natural environment for cooperation. This might also involve staff from student disability services. It might require an information technology person. Or it could mean that a teacher and a librarian would work together to solve a particular accessibility issue in an online course assignment. I have observed situations in which a faculty member felt awkward insisting that a student with a disability turn work in on schedule and wondering how much special allowance was deserved. The staff from student disability services has helped that faculty avoid being manipulated by the student.

If, for example, information technology staff became frustrated trying to help a student with a disability solve a technical issue with the LMS, a staff member from student disability services might be able to understand the student's problem and suggest a solution. Or the information technology staff might work with the teacher and persuade him or her to use (or avoid) certain LMS features. My experience with students with hearing impairments have helped me realize the usefulness of text chat for these students, but for someone who is blind, like me, text chat is very stressful. Faculty might want to use or avoid it depending on the complexion of a course. The more people with different insights work together, the better the solutions.

What Policies Will Guide the Team?

Although creating too many rules and regulations can create a bureaucratic atmosphere and undermine collegiality, putting a few policies and procedures down on paper will help clarify the purpose of the team and how it should function.

Crafting a mission statement is not a bad place to start. Base the team's purpose on institutional policies, such as its commitment to provide learning opportunities for everyone regardless of gender, religion, or disability. The policy should also be grounded in the new learning opportunities for students with disabilities created by modern information technologies. Although the policy should not intimidate people, it is appropriate to remind everyone that providing accessible online learning is a legal responsibility. Procedures should outline the operational specifics of who does what, and how those people might be held accountable.

THE ROLE OF STUDENT DISABILITY SERVICES

The staff of the department that is primarily concerned with serving students with disabilities in a face-to-face setting has also, in recent years, taken on the job of assisting those same students in using computers for their coursework. These staff members must have some understanding of the assistive software these students use, and they are usually able to provide the students with training on how to use it. If a student needs to use the Web for a class, training on using the assistive application for that purpose is also provided.

As a result, when students with disabilities become aware of inaccessible design features with the university's Web content, the staff members helping them also become aware of the inaccessibility of online content. The latter may even be the ones who take the complaint to the relevant campus department. All of this is to say that, even though this department's staff usually has no direct training on either Web accessibility issues or on online accessibility problems, their position has probably forced them to become concerned with it.

The interdepartmental nature of many online accessibility problems and solutions arises here again. For example, the Web designer may have little awareness of the needs of students with disabilities, and staff working with students with disabilities may know little about Web design. However, both bring unique awareness and specialized technical skills to the task and can therefore benefit from close cooperation.

Support for Online Students

As well as supporting students who attend classes on campus, student disabilities services staff are the obvious resource to assist online students with disabilities.

They have more familiarity with the personal and social issues faced by students with disabilities whether on campus or online. They will understand more about the assistive applications these students may be using than does anyone else. What they may lack is familiarity with the learning management system. This familiarity will put them in a position to provide support on how best to use the system by

- Giving tips to students with disabilities on how best to navigate the LMS and how to download and upload assignments

- Giving tips to teachers on LMS features that may be problematic and how to minimize them or how to work around them

- Reminding the administration to make accessibility a priority when purchasing a new LMS or when renewing its LMS contract

Providing Alternatives to Print Media

Although online learning primarily uses multimedia, images, and electronic text rather than print, many online courses still make significant use of print textbooks. Colleges and universities routinely provide textbooks in an alternative format for campus-based students with disabilities. This is usually done by the student disability services office, and it makes sense for the university to also have that department provide alternative texts to its online students.

In most cases this will mean providing the online student with an electronic version of the book. The two exceptions to providing students content in an electronic version is when a student requires math content in Nemeth Braille and when students need an alternative version of a complex diagram requiring hard-copy tactile graphics (see Chapter Six).

AWARENESS AND SKILLS TRAINING

The online learning accessibility support team should make sure that the training provided for new faculty includes content making them aware of the needs of students with disabilities for accessible online content and gives some initial training in how faculty can provide content that meets these requirements. Even faculty who are not teaching online courses will be offering some of their content in an electronic format, so this training is appropriate for on-campus as well as online instructors.

Training Workshops to Provide Online Accessibility

Training workshops on online accessibility should be designed with your campus in mind, including its departmental structure, its LMS, the technology skills of the online faculty, and the computer skills that you expect from the students. Some topics to consider include

- Describing the disability groups that need special support to use online learning.
- Demonstrating the assistive technologies these groups use to access online content.
- Demonstrating the strengths and weakness of the LMS in terms of accessibility.
- Providing hands-on training for faculty on how to create accessible content, including the special issues involved in math and science and in using multimedia.
- Providing training opportunities both in face-to-face and in online modules. Depending on the faculty, consider two training levels: one for those with little technical skill and another for those capable of using more advanced strategies.

Maintaining Awareness and Skills

Administrative memos sent to faculty should periodically include reminders of faculty's responsibility to create content with accessibility in mind. The team can use the learning management system's announcements to periodically post reminders. The team might consider a regular e-mail bulletin, which could provide a concrete accessibility tip and announcements of periodic training refresher opportunities. The bulletin should inform faculty of Web sites where more learning opportunities can be found, including accessibility-related Webinars.

The danger in a program that regularly reminds people of the need for accessibility is that it will be perceived as "nagging." Reminders should be extremely brief and avoid being negative. Be sure to include positive reminders as well, such as recognizing faculty who model creating accessible content and recognizing online students with disabilities for their achievements. The Delta Alpha Pi Honor Society is one way schools are highlighting the academic achievements of students with disabilities. It was founded by Dr. Edith Miller in 2004 at East Stroudsburg University of Pennsylvania.

ADMINISTRATION SUPPORT FOR ONLINE LEARNING

As mentioned earlier in the chapter, in addition to online learning being supported by a collegial, interdepartmental team, visible and strong support of the offices of the president and the provost for that team's work is crucial. Verbal support is important, but that endorsement must be backed up by decisions and action.

The president and the provost, or their representatives, should participate significantly on the support team—but not so much that they become dominant. Besides demonstrating administrative commitment, the administrative members can channel problems that come to the team back to the administration offices.

Legal Responsibility

The administration has, at minimum, the following five legal mandates related to providing online learning that is accessible to students with disabilities.

(Although it is common knowledge that Section 508 deals with Web standards, the first two items below relate to software requirements found in Section 508 standard, Subpart B—Technical Standards 1194.21 Software applications and operating systems.)

- Procure a learning management system that meets the demands of the ADA and of Section 508 of the Rehabilitation Act, or if that is not possible, discover how to provide reasonable accommodations for students with disabilities.

- Inform faculty and departments that when they procure commercial multimedia for class, they must purchase only accessible content.

- Provide adequate financing for online learning such that it is able to fulfill its commitment.

- Provide training for online faculty and related staff in how to create accessible online content and in how to interact with students with disabilities so that their experience meets the demands for timely delivery and provides a learning opportunity that is equal to that of other students.

- Be responsive to any student complaints that suggest (or state) that the institution is not fulfilling the mandates of the ADA and of the Rehabilitation Act.

ADA Compliance Office

The office in charge of ensuring compliance with the Americans with Disabilities Act serves as the institution's conscience in regard to students with disabilities. When other officials are swamped with competing demands and problems and might neglect the problems of these students, the ADA compliance officer can remind them of this obligation.

The officer must keep up on the law and its changing interpretations. In order to support online learning, the officer will need to become familiar with some of the technology it uses and understand the kinds of accessibility problems and solutions related to online students with disabilities.

Besides supporting the activities of the administration, faculty, and staff, the ADA compliance office is where the complaints of students with disabilities will be directed. If that office adopts a combative response, it may only lead to hostility. Conversely, if the office tries to hear and accommodate student complaints, the complaint will be resolved and not go any further.

Deciding when a complaint is genuinely unreasonable and should not be accepted can be problematic. Here is where a policy outlining student rights and responsibilities can be advantageous. Even when an investigating body such as the Office for Civil Rights disagrees with a policy, the fact that the school is thinking about accessibility and planning to achieve it will help blunt any criticism.

Financial Support

There is no one model for providing financial support for online learning. It has to grow out of each institution's unique culture and structures. I know of some institutions where the expenses are shared from the budgets of several related departments, and others where the online learning department has its own budget. One advantage of the latter model is it avoids interdepartmental turf wars.

TAKE-AWAYS FROM THIS BOOK

With the proliferation of new Internet-able devices such as smart phones, wireless laptops, Pads, Tablets, and Netbooks, we have all become awash in technology.

Now, more than ever before, we need to think of online learning as being about students, not just technology.

Frequently, faculty and staff worry that providing accessibility in online learning for students with disabilities will be difficult and interfere with providing quality learning for others. This book has endeavored to show that neither of those fears is valid and that—to the contrary—including students with disabilities in online learning is a challenging and exciting opportunity. If I have done my job successfully, you will take away the following points from having read this book:

- The accessibility of an online learning system depends on the accessibility of the learning management system, the accessibility of the course content, the quality of the student's adaptive technology, and the student's skill in using it.

- The first step in advancing online content accessibility is improving your quality of teaching and the clarity of your communication for everyone, including students with disabilities.

- Although creating accessible content has frequently been presented as a complex, technical challenge of mastering HTML code, applying universal design principles in the use of familiar authoring tools is not a burden and results in reasonably accessible output.

- Creating math content that is accessible is rapidly becoming feasible and adds little work for the author of scientific content.

- Although graphics and charts still present serious barriers, faculty may be able to get help in providing them to students with disabilities in the form of hard-copy tactile graphics.

- Multimedia is becoming easier to create and has been proven to be a valuable enrichment to course content. Providing captioned video is now less a technical problem and mostly an issue of patiently transcribing the presentation.

Creating an online learning system involves several departments and several specialties, and when it is being made accessible for students with disabilities, the number of support staff needed increases. If, as they say, it takes a village to raise a child, it takes a campuswide support team to provide an effective, equal learning experience for these students.

Finally, remember that when you have a student with a disability in your course, it's vital that you focus on that student's ability—not on the disability. Online learning gives these students opportunities that outweigh their disabilities. And as a teacher, it gives you the potential to contribute to the most level learning space in history for students with disabilities. The choice of whether you realize that potential is yours.

APPENDIX A: SECTION 508 WEB STANDARDS

1194.22 Web-based intranet and Internet information and applications. Sixteen rules. Accessed February 19, 2010.

SECTION 508 STANDARDS, SUBPART B—TECHNICAL STANDARDS

(a) A text equivalent for every non-text element shall be provided (e.g., via "alt," "longdesc," or in element content).

(b) Equivalent alternatives for any multimedia presentation shall be synchronized with the presentation.

(c) Web pages shall be designed so that all information conveyed with color is also available without color, for example from context or markup.

(d) Documents shall be organized so they are readable without requiring an associated style sheet.

(e) Redundant text links shall be provided for each active region of a server-side image map.

(f) Client-side image maps shall be provided instead of server-side image maps except where the regions cannot be defined with an available geometric shape.

(g) Row and column headers shall be identified for data tables.

Excerpted from the Section 508 Web site and from the page at http://www.section508.gov/index.cfm?FuseAction=content&ID=12.

(h) Markup shall be used to associate data cells and header cells for data tables that have two or more logical levels of row or column headers.

(i) Frames shall be titled with text that facilitates frame identification and navigation.

(j) Pages shall be designed to avoid causing the screen to flicker with a frequency greater than 2 Hz and lower than 55 Hz.

(k) A text-only page, with equivalent information or functionality, shall be provided to make a Web site comply with the provisions of this part, when compliance cannot be accomplished in any other way. The content of the text-only page shall be updated whenever the primary page changes.

(l) When pages utilize scripting languages to display content, or to create interface elements, the information provided by the script shall be identified with functional text that can be read by assistive technology.

(m) When a Web page requires that an applet, plug-in, or other application be present on the client system to interpret page content, the page must provide a link to a plug-in or applet that complies with §1194.21(a) through (l).

(n) When electronic forms are designed to be completed on-line, the form shall allow people using assistive technology to access the information, field elements, and functionality required for completion and submission of the form, including all directions and cues.

(o) A method shall be provided that permits users to skip repetitive navigation links.

(p) When a timed response is required, the user shall be alerted and given sufficient time to indicate more time is required.

APPENDIX B: WEBAIM SUMMARY OF W3C WAI WCAG 2

This is taken from the WebAIM site at http://www.webaim.org/standards/wcag/checklist.

IMPORTANT!

The following is NOT the Web Content Accessibility Guidelines (WCAG) 2.0. It is, however, a simple checklist that presents our recommendations for implementing HTML-related principles and techniques for those seeking WCAG 2.0 conformance. The language used here is significantly different from the official WCAG 2.0 specification (http://www.w3.org/TR/WCAG20/) to make it more easily implemented and verified for web pages.

Guidelines for Using This Checklist:

- This checklist **cannot be used to verify conformance with WCAG 2.0.** You must reference official WCAG 2.0 documentation to determine any level of conformance or non-conformance.

- This checklist **should not be referenced in policies or in policy adoption**. While this is a useful resource for technical implementation of WCAG for HTML content, it is not a useful policy checklist. Official WCAG 2.0 documentation provides much better mechanisms for implementing accessibility into policy or law.

- WCAG 2.0 covers accessibility of all web content and is not technology specific. The language of this checklist has been targeted **primarily for evaluation**

of HTML content. It is, therefore, fairly limited and subject to technology changes, whereas WCAG 2.0 is much less so.

- This checklist contains **WebAIM's interpretation of WCAG guidelines and success criteria and our own recommended techniques for satisfying those success criteria**. The first column of the table below links to the official WCAG 2.0 success criteria. Only the official guidelines can be used for verifying conformance with WCAG 2.0.

A PDF version of this checklist is also available (download Adobe Reader).

PERCEIVABLE: WEB CONTENT IS MADE AVAILABLE TO THE SENSES—SIGHT, HEARING, AND/OR TOUCH

Guideline 1.1	
Text Alternatives: Provide text alternatives for any non-text content	
SUCCESS CRITERIA	**WEBAIM'S RECOMMENDATIONS**
1.1.1 Non-text Content (Level A)	• All images, form image buttons, and image map hot spots have appropriate, equivalent alternative text.
	• Images that do not convey content, are decorative, or with content that is already conveyed in text are given null alt text (alt="") or implemented as CSS backgrounds. All linked images have descriptive alternative text.
	• Equivalent alternatives to complex images are provided in context or on a separate (linked and/or referenced via longdesc) page.
	• Form buttons have a descriptive value.
	• Form inputs have associated text labels or, if labels cannot be used, a descriptive title attribute.
	• Embedded multimedia is identified via accessible text.
	• Frames are appropriately titled.

Guideline 1.2
Time-based Media: Provide alternatives for time-based media

SUCCESS CRITERIA	WEBAIM'S RECOMMENDATIONS
1.2.1 Prerecorded Audio-only and Video-only (Level A)	• A descriptive text transcript (including all relevant visual and auditory clues and indicators) is provided for non-live, web-based audio (audio podcasts, MP3 files, etc.). • A text or audio description is provided for non-live, web-based video-only (e.g., video that has no audio track).
1.2.2 Captions (Prerecorded) (Level A)	• Synchronized captions are provided for non-live, web-based video (YouTube videos, etc.).
1.2.3 Audio Description or Media Alternative (Prerecorded) (Level A)	• A descriptive text transcript OR audio description audio track is provided for non-live, web-based video.
1.2.4 Captions (Live) (Level AA)	• Synchronized captions are provided for all live multimedia that contains audio (audio-only broadcasts, web casts, video conferences, Flash animations, etc.).
1.2.5 Audio Description (Prerecorded) (Level AA)	• Audio descriptions are provided for all video content NOTE: Only required if the video conveys content visually that is not available in the default audio track.
1.2.6 Sign Language (Prerecorded) (Level AAA)	• A sign language video is provided for all media content that contains audio.
1.2.7 Extended Audio Description (Prerecorded) (Level AAA)	• When an audio description track cannot be added to video due to audio timing (e.g., no pauses in the audio), an alternative version of the video with pauses that allow audio descriptions is provided.

Continued

SUCCESS CRITERIA	WEBAIM'S RECOMMENDATIONS
1.2.8 Media Alternative (Prerecorded) (Level AAA)	• A descriptive text transcript is provided for all pre-recorded media that has a video track.
1.2.9 Audio-only (Live) (Level AAA)	• A descriptive text transcript (e.g., the script of the live audio) is provided for all live content that has audio.

NOTE: If the audio or video is designated as an alternative to web content (an audio or sign language version of a web page, for example), then the web content itself serves as the alternative.

Guideline 1.3
Adaptable: Create content that can be presented in different ways (for example simpler layout) without losing information or structure

SUCCESS CRITERIA	WEBAIM'S RECOMMENDATIONS
1.3.1 Info and Relationships (Level A)	• Semantic markup is used to designate headings (<h1>), lists (<ul>, <ol>, and <dl>), emphasized or special text (<strong>, <code>, <abbr>, <blockquote>, for example), etc. Semantic markup is used appropriately.
	• Tables are used for tabular data. Where necessary, data cells are associated with their headers. Data table captions and summaries are used where appropriate.
	• Text labels are associated with form input elements. Related form elements are grouped with fieldset/legend.
1.3.2 Meaningful Sequence (Level A)	• The reading and navigation order (determined by code order) is logical and intuitive.

SUCCESS CRITERIA	WEBAIM'S RECOMMENDATIONS
1.3.3 Sensory Characteristics (Level A)	• Instructions do not rely upon shape, size, or visual location (e.g., "Click the square icon to continue" or "Instructions are in the right-hand column"). • Instructions do not rely upon sound (e.g., "A beeping sound indicates you may continue").

Guideline 1.4
Distinguishable: Make it easier for users to see and hear content including separating foreground from background

SUCCESS CRITERIA	WEBAIM'S RECOMMENDATIONS
1.4.1 Use of Color (Level A)	• Color is not used as the sole method of conveying content or distinguishing visual elements. • Color alone is not used to distinguish links from surrounding text unless the luminance contrast between the link and the surrounding text is at least 3:1 and an additional differentiation (e.g., it becomes underlined) is provided when the link is hovered over or receives focus.
1.4.2 Audio Control (Level A)	• A mechanism is provided to stop, pause, mute, or adjust volume for audio that automatically plays on a page for more than 3 seconds.
1.4.3 Contrast (Minimum) (Level AA)	• Text and images of text have a contrast ratio of at least 4.5:1. • Large text (over 18 point or 14 point bold) has a contrast ratio of at least 3:1.

Continued

SUCCESS CRITERIA	WEBAIM'S RECOMMENDATIONS
1.4.4 Resize text (Level AA)	• The page is readable and functional when the text size is doubled.
1.4.5 Images of Text (Level AA)	• If the same visual presentation can be made using text alone, an image is not used to present that text.
1.4.6 Contrast (Enhanced) (Level AAA)	• Text and images of text have a contrast ratio of at least 7:1.
	• Large text (over 18 point or 14 point bold) has a contrast ratio of at least 4.5:1.
1.4.7 Low or No Background Audio (Level AAA)	• Audio of speech has no or very low background noise so the speech is easily distinguished.
1.4.8 Visual Presentation (Level AAA)	• Blocks of text over one sentence in length:
	• Are no more than 80 characters wide.
	• Are NOT fully justified (aligned to both the left and the right margins).
	• Have adequate line spacing (at least 1/2 the height of the text) and paragraph spacing (1.5 times line spacing).
	• Have a specified foreground and background color. These can be applied to specific elements or to the page as a whole using CSS (and thus inherited by all other elements).
	• Do NOT require horizontal scrolling when the text size is doubled.
1.4.9 Images of Text (No Exception) (Level AAA)	• Text is used within an image only for decoration (image does not convey content) OR when the information cannot be presented with text alone.

OPERABLE: INTERFACE FORMS, CONTROLS, AND NAVIGATION ARE OPERABLE

Guideline 2.1
Keyboard Accessible: Make all functionality available from a keyboard

SUCCESS CRITERIA	WEBAIM'S RECOMMENDATIONS
2.1.1 Keyboard (Level A)	• All page functionality is available using the keyboard, unless the functionality cannot be accomplished in any known way using a keyboard (e.g., free hand drawing).
	• Page-specified shortcut keys and accesskeys (accesskey should typically be avoided) do not conflict with existing browser and screen reader shortcuts.
2.1.2 No Keyboard Trap (Level A)	• Keyboard focus is never locked or trapped at one particular page element. The user can navigate to and from all navigable page elements using only a keyboard.
2.1.3 Keyboard (No Exception) (Level AAA)	• All page functionality is available using the keyboard.

Guideline 2.2
Enough Time: Provide users enough time to read and use content

SUCCESS CRITERIA	WEBAIM'S RECOMMENDATIONS
2.2.1 Timing Adjustable (Level A)	• If a page or application has a time limit, the user is given options to turn off, adjust, or extend that time limit. This is not a requirement for real-time events (e.g., an auction), where the time limit is absolutely required, or if the time limit is longer than 20 hours.
2.2.2 Pause, Stop, Hide (Level A)	• Automatically moving, blinking, or scrolling content that lasts longer than 3 seconds can be paused, stopped, or hidden by the user. Moving, blinking, or scrolling can be used to draw attention to or highlight content as long as it lasts less than 3 seconds.
	• Automatically updating content (e.g., automatically redirecting or refreshing a page, a news ticker, AJAX updated field, a notification alert, etc.) can be paused, stopped, or hidden by the user or the user can manually control the timing of the updates.
2.2.3 No Timing (Level AAA)	• The content and functionality has no time limits or constraints.
2.2.4 Interruptions (Level AAA)	• Interruptions (alerts, page updates, etc.) can be postponed or suppressed by the user.
2.2.5 Re-authenticating (Level AAA)	• If an authentication session expires, the user can re-authenticate and continue the activity without losing any data from the current page.

Guideline 2.3
Seizures: Do not design content in a way that is known to cause seizures

SUCCESS CRITERIA	WEBAIM'S RECOMMENDATIONS
2.3.1 Three Flashes or Below Threshold (Level A)	• No page content flashes more than 3 times per second unless that flashing content is sufficiently small and the flashes are of low contrast and do not contain too much red. (See general flash and red flash thresholds.)
2.3.2 Three Flashes (Level AAA)	• No page content flashes more than 3 times per second.

Guideline 2.4
Navigable: Provide ways to help users navigate, find content, and determine where they are

SUCCESS CRITERIA	WEBAIM'S RECOMMENDATIONS
2.4.1 Bypass Blocks (Level A)	• A link is provided to skip navigation and other page elements that are repeated across web pages.
	• If a page has a proper heading structure, this may be considered a sufficient technique instead of a "Skip to main content" link. Note that navigating by headings is not yet supported in all browsers.
	• If a page uses frames and the frames are appropriately titled, this is a sufficient technique for bypassing individual frames.
2.4.2 Page Titled (Level A)	• The web page has a descriptive and informative page title.
2.4.3 Focus Order (Level A)	• The navigation order of links, form elements, etc., is logical and intuitive.

Continued

SUCCESS CRITERIA	WEBAIM'S RECOMMENDATIONS
2.4.4 Link Purpose (In Context) (Level A)	• The purpose of each link (or form image button or image map hotspot) can be determined from the link text alone, or from the link text and its context (e.g., surrounding paragraph, list item, table cell, or table headers).
	• Links (or form image buttons) with the same text that go to different locations are readily distinguishable.
2.4.5 Multiple Ways (Level AA)	• Multiple ways are available to find other web pages on the site—at least two of: a list of related pages, table of contents, site map, site search, or list of all available web pages.
2.4.6 Headings and Labels (Level AA)	• Page headings and labels for form and interactive controls are informative. Avoid duplicating heading (e.g., "More Details") or label text (e.g., "First Name") unless the structure provides adequate differentiation between them.
2.4.7 Focus Visible (Level AA)	• It is visually apparent which page element has the current keyboard focus (i.e., as you tab through the page, you can see where you are).
2.4.8 Location (Level AAA)	• If a web page is part of a sequence of pages or within a complex site structure, an indication of the current page location is provided, for example, through breadcrumbs or specifying the current step in a sequence (e.g., "Step 2 of 5—Shipping Address").
2.4.9 Link Purpose (Link Only) (Level AAA)	• The purpose of each link (or form image button or image map hotspot) can be determined from the link text alone.
	• There are no links (or form image buttons) with the same text that go to different locations.
2.4.10 Section Headings (Level AAA)	• Beyond providing an overall document structure, individual sections of content are designated using headings, where appropriate.

UNDERSTANDABLE: CONTENT AND INTERFACE ARE UNDERSTANDABLE

Guideline 3.1
Readable: Make text content readable and understandable

SUCCESS CRITERIA	WEBAIM'S RECOMMENDATIONS
3.1.1 Language of Page (Level A)	• The language of the page is identified using the HTML lang attribute (<html lang="en">, for example).
3.1.2 Language of Parts (Level AA)	• When appropriate, the language of sections of content that are a different language are identified, for example, by using the lang attribute (<blockquote lang="es">).
3.1.3 Unusual Words (Level AAA)	• Words that may be ambiguous, unknown, or used in a very specific way are defined through adjacent text, a definition list, a glossary, or other suitable method.
3.1.4 Abbreviations (Level AAA)	• Expansions for abbreviations are provided by expanding or explaining the definition the first time it is used, using the <abbr> element, or linking to a definition or glossary. NOTE: WCAG 2.0 gives no exception for regularly understood abbreviations (e.g., "HTML" on a web design site must always be expanded).
3.1.5 Reading Level (Level AAA)	• A more understandable alternative is provided for content that is more advanced than can be reasonably read by a person with roughly 9 years of primary education.
3.1.6 Pronunciation (Level AAA)	• If the pronunciation of a word is vital to understanding that word, its pronunciation is provided immediately following the word or via a link or glossary.

Guideline 3.2
Predictable: Make Web pages appear and operate in predictable ways

SUCCESS CRITERIA	WEBAIM'S RECOMMENDATIONS
3.2.1 On Focus (Level A)	• When a page element receives focus, it does not result in a substantial change to the page, the spawning of a pop-up window, an additional change of keyboard focus, or any other change that could confuse or disorient the user.
3.2.2 On Input (Level A)	• When a user inputs information or interacts with a control, it does not result in a substantial change to the page, the spawning of a pop-up window, an additional change of keyboard focus, or any other change that could confuse or disorient the user unless the user is informed of the change ahead of time.
3.2.3 Consistent Navigation (Level AA)	• Navigation links that are repeated on web pages do not change order when navigating through the site.
3.2.4 Consistent Identification (Level AA)	• Elements that have the same functionality across multiple web pages are consistently identified. For example, a search box at the top of the site should always be labeled the same way.
3.2.5 Change on Request (Level AAA)	• Substantial changes to the page, the spawning of pop-up windows, uncontrolled changes of keyboard focus, or any other change that could confuse or disorient the user must be initiated by the user. Alternatively, the user is provided an option to disable such changes.

Guideline 3.3
Input Assistance: Help users avoid and correct mistakes

SUCCESS CRITERIA	WEBAIM'S RECOMMENDATIONS
3.3.1 Error Identification (Level A)	• Required form elements or form elements that require a specific format, value, or length provide this information within the element's label (or if a label is not provided, within the element's title attribute). • If utilized, form validation cues and errors (client-side or server-side) alert users to errors in an efficient, intuitive, and accessible manner. The error is clearly identified, quick access to the problematic element is provided, and user is allowed to easily fix the error and resubmit the form.
3.3.2 Labels or Instructions (Level A)	• Sufficient labels, cues, and instructions for required interactive elements are provided via instructions, examples, properly positioned form labels, and/or fieldsets/legends.
3.3.3 Error Suggestion (Level AA)	• If an input error is detected (via client-side or server-side validation), provide suggestions for fixing the input in a timely and accessible manner.
3.3.4 Error Prevention (Legal, Financial, Data) (Level AA)	• If the user can change or delete legal, financial, or test data, the changes/deletions are reversible, verified, or confirmed.
3.3.5 Help (Level AAA)	• Provide instructions and cues in context to help in form completion and submission.
3.3.6 Error Prevention (All) (Level AAA)	• If the user can submit information, the submission is reversible, verified, or confirmed.

ROBUST: CONTENT CAN BE USED RELIABLY BY A WIDE VARIETY OF USER AGENTS, INCLUDING ASSISTIVE TECHNOLOGIES

Guideline 4.1
Compatible: Maximize compatibility with current and future user agents, including assistive technologies

SUCCESS CRITERIA	WEBAIM'S RECOMMENDATIONS
4.1.1 Parsing (Level A)	• Significant HTML/XHTML validation/parsing errors are avoided. Check at http://validator.w3.org/.
4.1.2 Name, Role, Value (Level A)	• Markup is used in a way that facilitates accessibility. This includes following the HTML/XHTML specifications and using forms, form labels, frame titles, etc., appropriately.

APPENDIX C: AMERICAN FOUNDATION FOR THE BLIND'S DISTANCE LEARNING SURVEY

DISTANCE LEARNING: HOW ACCESSIBLE ARE ONLINE EDUCATIONAL TOOLS

More and more schools, colleges and universities are using online educational tools that students are required to use to obtain course syllabi, access lectures and associated material, participate in class discussions, read course material, and receive grades and feedback from instructors. These popular tools, such as Blackboard, can frequently pose significant barriers to students with vision loss because they do not work well, if at all, with computer programs commonly used by students who are blind or visually impaired to access content displayed on the computer screen. For example, screen reading software reads the contents of the screen aloud. Screen magnification software enlarges text and graphics displayed on the computer screen in a customized way.

Findings from the American Foundation for the Blind (AFB) distance learning survey indicated the most important and necessary features of online educational tools presented significant problems for those using assistive technology such as screen reading or screen magnification software. Nearly one third of respondents who used assistive technology to access online educational tools reported the experiences as unreliable/inconsistent or no successful use/access. Open ended questions gave respondents the opportunity to share their personal

Reproduced here with permission of the author, American Foundation for the Blind Public Policy Center, 1660 L Street, N.W., Suite 513, Washington, D.C., 20036, (202)-822–0830, www.afb.org/policy.

stories. In nearly every instance, respondents indicated features that were inaccessible.

METHODOLOGY

AFB explored ways in which popular online educational tools can be made more accessible with the help of nearly 100 individuals who voluntarily completed an informal online questionnaire. Three open ended questions assessed the types of online educational tools with which people had experience, the features that seemed to be usable, the features that posed the most problems, and the access technology, such as screen reading or screen magnification software, that people used to access online tools.

Respondents were also asked to provide an accessibility rating for online educational tools with which they had experience. To do so, respondents completed a Likert item that asked, "On a scale of 1 to 5, how accessible/usable do you think these tools are?" with response options 1 = no successful use/access, 2 = unreliable/inconsistent, 3 = doable with patience/effort, 4 = fairly usable with some quirks, and 5 = accessible without difficulty.

Even though the survey did not explicitly ask for such information, respondents offered several suggestions about how to best accommodate for many of the inaccessible features.

RESULTS

Respondents included students who have used online educational tools and family members of such students as well as teachers and university faculty who had substantial experience and expertise with such online tools. Each of these respondents willingly shared their stories and, in doing so, helped inform the findings included in this special report.

Survey participants commented on a variety of online education tools including Blackboard, Web CT, Live Text, Moodle, Apex Learning, Aventa, MyMathLab, Wimba, ed2go, Elluminate, PowerSchool, and other various online educational tools available exclusively through certain educational programs. The most frequently addressed forum was Blackboard. Approximately 70% of respondents commented on Blackboard either exclusively or in combination with their thoughts about other online educational tools. Thus, Blackboard was the most commonly used online educational tool involved in this survey.

Table C.1
Percentage of Respondents Who Provided Accessibility Ratings of Online Education Tools by Type of Online Educational Tool

ACCESSIBILITY RATING	OVERALL	BLACKBOARD	WEB CT	LIVE TEXT	OTHER
1. No successful use/access	6%	4%	0%	67%	7%
2. Unreliable/ inconsistent	24%	15%	50%	33%	50%
3. Doable with patience/effort	30%	34%	50%	0%	7%
4. Fairly usable with some quirks	31%	38%	0%	0%	22%
5. Accessible without difficulty	9%	9%	0%	0%	14%

The results from the Likert item that evaluated accessibility and usability are provided in table format. Table C.1 is organized by accessibility rating value and type of online educational tool. The percentages of responses for each of the five possible rating values are shown. Overall percentages are provided as well as percentages for each type of online educational tool with the most substantial responses. When there were not substantial responses for a particular online educational tool, the response for that particular online educational tool was designated as other. The category designated as other included Moodle, Apex Learning, Aventa, MyMathLab, Wimba, ed2go, Elluminate, PowerSchool, and other various online educational tools available exclusively through certain educational programs.

The overall accessibility rating showed that people who used screen reading or screen magnification software rarely accessed online educational tools without difficulty. On the other hand, the overall accessibility rating also showed that people who use screen reading or screen magnification software were rarely completely unable to use online educational tools. Thus, the overall results demonstrated that responses fell somewhere in between the best and worst extremes with more than 80% of respondents who use assistive technology to access online educational tools reporting the experience to be either fairly usable with some quirks, doable with patience/effort, or unreliable/inconsistent.

The accessibility rating was considered by type of online educational tool. Nearly 20% of the respondents rated their Blackboard experience as unreliable/ inconsistent or no successful use/access. Since 70% of respondents commented on Blackboard either exclusively or in combination with their thoughts about other online educational tools, any online education tool other than Blackboard was not considered widely used by those who responded to this survey. The online educational tools that were the least widely used demonstrated at least half of respondents rated their accessibility experience no better than unreliable/ inconsistent. This included 50% of those who used Web CT, 100% of those who used Live Text, and 57% of those who used other online educational tools. Thus, the results showed that the least commonly used online educational tools were also the most troublesome for people with vision loss who use assistive technology to access online education.

Table C.2 shows the accessibility rating valued organized by the type of assistive technology respondents reported that they used. The type of assistive technology respondents used was organized as either screen reading software or screen magnification software.

Of the respondents that reported the type of assistive technology they used to access online educational tools, 85% reported that they used some type of screen

Table C.2
Percentage of Respondents Who Provided Accessibility Ratings of Online Educational Tools by Type of Assistive Technology Used

ACCESSIBILITY RATING	SCREEN READING SOFTWARE %	SCREEN MAGNIFICATION SOFTWARE %
1. No successful use/access	5%	18%
2. Unreliable/inconsistent	25%	45%
3. Doable with patience/effort	30%	27%
4. Fairly usable with some quirks	33%	9%
5. Accessible without difficulty	7%	0%

reading software and 15% used some type of screen magnification software. The data showed that 30% of those who used screen reading software to access online educational tools reported the experience as unreliable/inconsistent or no successful use/access compared with 63% of those who used screen magnification software. Respondents showed, therefore, that those using screen magnification software were more inclined to have a less successful experience accessing online educational tools than those using screen reading software.

In addition to the survey items discussed thus far, one of the open ended questions asked participants to describe the kinds of difficulties experienced when using these tools.

Participants were asked, "What features seem to be usable?" and "What features pose the most problems?" for this open ended item. There were significantly more responses that indicated inaccessible experiences than there were discussions of usable features. In a few instances, certain features were noted as being both problematic and usable depending on the respondent. The use of HTML content when written with proper structure was the only usable feature that was not also mentioned as a problematic feature.

This report highlights the problematic features in table format. Table C.3 shows the problematic features of various online educational tools. Table C.4 shows the problematic features of online educational tools organized by the type of assistive technology respondents reported that they used. The type of assistive technology respondents reported that they used was categorized as either screen reading software or screen magnification software.

The results in Table C.4 demonstrated that users of screen reading and screen magnification software both experienced many significant problems accessing important features of online educational tools. Those who used screen reading software, the most commonly used type of assistive technology tool involved in this survey, experienced slightly more problems than those using screen magnification software.

As mentioned, the survey did not ask for suggestions about how to best accommodate for many of the most problematic features that people who have vision loss experience with online educational tools. Several respondents provided this useful information anyhow. Many of these suggestions do not involve any drastic measures but instead rely on the proactive role of online learning designers or instructors.

Table C.3
Problematic Features of Online Educational Tools by
Type of Online Educational Tool

PROBLEMATIC FEATURES	BLACKBOARD	WEB CT	LIVE TEXT	OTHER
Assessments	Yes	Yes	Yes	Yes
Assignments	Yes	Yes	Yes	Yes
Attachments	Yes	No	Yes	No
Real-time chat feature	Yes	Yes	No	Yes
Color contrast	Yes	No	Yes	Yes
Discussion board	Yes	Yes	No	No
Documents	Yes	Yes	Yes	Yes
E-mail	Yes	Yes	No	Yes
Graphics	Yes	No	No	Yes
Maintenance	Yes	No	No	Yes
Modifying text	Yes	No	No	No
Navigation	Yes	Yes	Yes	Yes
Recordings	Yes	No	No	No
Security	Yes	Yes	Yes	Yes
Sighted assistance required	Yes	Yes	Yes	Yes
Technical support	Yes	Yes	Yes	No
Timed graded activities	Yes	No	No	Yes
Training	Yes	No	No	Yes
Videos	Yes	No	No	Yes

Note: "Yes" indicates the feature was problematic for that particular type of online educational tool. "No" indicates the feature was not problematic for that particular type of online educational tool.

Suggestions for how to deal with the most problematic features of online educational tools for people with vision loss are provided below.

- Respondents frequently noted that chat features and assessments that involved matching were not compatible with access software. Until this situation is remedied, online learning designers should plan courses so that students only use features that are truly accessible and, in doing so, do not use synchronous

Table C.4
Problematic Features of Online Educational Tools by Type of Assistive Technology Used

PROBLEMATIC FEATURES	SCREEN READING SOFTWARE	SCREEN MAGNIFICATION SOFTWARE
Assessments	Yes	Yes
Assignments	Yes	Yes
Attachments	Yes	No
Real-time chat feature	Yes	Yes
Color contrast	No	Yes
Discussion board	Yes	Yes
Documents	Yes	Yes
E-mail	Yes	Yes
Graphics	Yes	No
Maintenance	Yes	No
Modifying text	No	Yes
Navigation	Yes	Yes
Recordings	Yes	No
Security	Yes	No
Sighted assistance required	Yes	Yes
Technical support	Yes	Yes
Timed graded activities	Yes	Yes
Training	Yes	Yes
Videos	Yes	Yes

Note: "Yes" indicates the feature was problematic for that particular type of assistive technology. "No" indicates the feature was not problematic for that particular type of assistive technology.

chat rooms or assessments that involve matching. Only asynchronous features should be used as well as assessments that do not involve matching.

• When timed assessments are not necessary, it is recommended that timed assessments are not implemented. When time assessments are necessary, instructors can provide students with vision loss extended time. One respondent who used screen magnification software to access an online educational tool explained that timed tests were difficult to use for a few reasons. The screen did not magnify very well. It took her a long time to find everything on the screen to read and choose from. By the time everything was read and answered, the time was severely lessened. When she was not being timed, the program was not as difficult to use because she could take her time.

- Online learning designers who use consistent designs, proper headings, fewer frames, contrasting colors, accessible graphics, as well as other formatting techniques can make problematic features of online education more accessible for students using assistive technology. A large part of how accessible various features are within online educational tools depends on how the instructor designs, organizes, and maintains the course. For example, students with vision loss reported that they were unable to access exam tools because of the inconsistent design of this feature within the same online course.

- Instructors should post all materials as Microsoft Word documents and PDF files. PDF files were often reported as problematic for accessibility with screen reading and screen magnification software. In these instances, students with vision loss were unable to access required readings in PDF file format and would have been able to access the required reading materials if they were posted in Microsoft Word documents.

- Instructors should ask students to share accessibility concerns so the instructors can attempt to remedy the concerns. Some educational programs have hired consultants to try out any new features or versions to try to anticipate problems and solutions. This technique is highly recommended.

- Online systems have regular maintenance that should be limited in how often it occurs and the significance of the updates. Students with vision loss explained the difficulty they encountered when changes were made to the system.

- Several respondents advocated for better inclusion of assistive technology specialists when educational programs make decisions about online learning systems.

- Whenever possible, students with vision loss should frequently save their work in computer programs and documents that are independent of the online course. This is in an effort to back-up and retrieve work that students reported often gets lost when they would inadvertently be knocked out of exams or assignments. In other cases, students took this proactive role because work they submitted through the online educational tool was not received by the instructor due to technical problems.

- It is often more feasible to e-mail instructors directly from regularly used e-mail providers rather than from within the e-mail feature of the online educational tools. Students with vision loss reported that they took a proactive role in this effort by acquiring their instructor's e-mail addresses at the onset of the course and advocating their need for this accommodation.

- Becoming very familiar with the shortcut keystrokes for certain online educational tools can be beneficial for students using access software.

- Students with vision loss should keep their access software as up-to-date as possible so that the latest updates are available to them.

DISCUSSION

Overall results demonstrated that nearly one third of respondents who use assistive technology to access online educational tools reported the experience as unreliable/inconsistent or no successful use/access. Open ended questions gave respondents the opportunity to share their personal stories. Data indicated that several of the most important features of online educational tools posed the most problems for those who used screen reading or screen magnification software. In nearly every instance, respondents indicated features that were inaccessible.

The ability of respondents to effectively use access technology was considered in this report. As mentioned, respondents included students who have used online educational tools, family members of such students, as well as teachers and university faculty who had substantial experience and expertise with such online tools. Consistent trends among participant responses were substantial enough to negate this otherwise potentially salient factor.

Even though the survey did not ask for suggestions about how to best accommodate for many of the most problematic features that people who have vision loss experience with online education, respondents provided suggestions. Those involved with online education are encouraged to adhere to the aforementioned suggestions and those who have the potential to develop the technical expertise to better the situation are urged to resolve many of the problematic features. It is noted that adhering to these suggestions can give students with vision loss a better chance for successful access with the usable features of online education until the problematic features are remedied by the necessary experts. It is also noted that adhering to these suggestions can give all students a notable better chance for successful online education experiences.

Efforts to remedy the situation should be grounded in bettering the problematic features that prevent full and equal access for people with vision loss. Respondents shared their personal stories through the open ended questions included in this survey. Inaccessible real-time chat features prevent students with vision loss from earning points required for class participation. Sighted parents must access online education materials for their high school children with vision loss. University students with vision loss are unable to complete postsecondary degrees that involve the use of online educational tools due to accessibility barriers that are too substantial to overcome. These are unacceptable circumstances in this time of technological prominence when computers have the capacity to bridge the digital divide.

Prepared November 2008

REFERENCES

American Foundation for the Blind (November 2008). "Distance Learning: How Accessible Are Online Educational Tools." [Online Publication]. Retrieved from http://www.afb.org/Section.asp?SectionID=3&TopicID=138&DocumentID=4492. Accessed June 27, 2009.

Bailey, B. (November, 2001). "Multimedia and Learning." Retrieved from http://www.webusability.com/article_multimedia_and_learning_11_2001.htm. Accessed July 25, 2009.

Center for Applied Special Technology (CAST) (2010). "What Is Universal Design for Learning?" [Online Publication]. Retrieved from http://www.cast.org/research/udl/index.html. Accessed: February 18, 2010.

Center for Universal Design (2008). "About UD." [Online Publication]. Retrieved from http://design.ncsu.edu/cud/about_ud/about_ud.htm. Accessed February 18, 2010.

Clark, R. (2007). "Leveraging Multimedia for Learning" [Online Publication]. Retrieved from www.adobe.com/products/captivate/_leveraging_multimedia.pdf. Accessed July 18, 2009.

Dennett, J., Earl, S., Kaplan, D., Petri, K., Rangin, H., & Thompson, T. (2008). "Accessibility of Learning Management Systems." Panel Presentation from 11th Annual Accessing Higher Ground Accessible Media, Web & Technology Conference 2008. Boulder, Colorado.

DO-IT Video (1994). "Working Together: Faculty and Students with Disabilities." Video produced by DO-IT, a project at the University of Washington. Available http://www.washington.edu/doit/Video/wt_fac.html. Accessed February 24, 2010.

Friedman, T. (2005). *The World Is Flat: A Brief History of the Twenty-first Century*. New York: Farrar, Straus & Giroux.

Gardner, J. (1996). "Tactile Graphics: An Overview and Resource Guide." *Information Technology and Disability Journal*, Vol. 3. [Online Publication]. Available http://people.rit.edu/easi/itd/itdv03n4/article2.htm. Accessed February 24, 2010.

Jones, R. (1994). "Math and Science Symposium at Recording for the Blind." *Information Technology and Disability Journal*, Vol. 3. [Online Publication]. Available http://people.erit.edu/easi/itd/itdv01n4/article1.htm. Accessed February 24, 2010.

Kaplan, D. E-mail message to author. January 17, 2010.

Kubiak-Becker, E., & Dick, T. (1996). "A Brief Historical Overview of Tactile and Auditory Aids for Visually Impaired Mathematics Educators and Students." *Information Technology and Disability Journal*, Vol. 3. [Online Publication]. Available http://people.rit.edu/easi/itd/itdv03n1/article2.htm. Accessed: February 24, 2010.

Mack, C. (1993). "Teaching Blind Students to Use Tactile Displays." [Online] Available: http://people.rit.edu/easi/easisem/magar.html. Accessed February 25, 2010.

National Center on Universal Design for Learning. (2010). "UDL Guidelines—Version 1.0." [Online Publication]. Retrieved from http://www.udlcenter.org/aboutudl/udlguidelines. Accessed: February 18, 2010.

Nemeth, A. (1995). E-mail message to Members of the R & D and the S & E committees of NFB. "Mathspeak." August 5, 1995. Available http://www.nfbcal.org/nfb-rd/0713.html. Accessed February 24, 2010.

Nemeth, A. (1996). "Teaching Mathematics as a Blind Person." Presentation to the Mathematical Association of America, Orlando, FL. January 10, 1996. Available http://www.people.rit.edu/easi/easisem/nemeth1.htm. Accessed February 24, 2010.

Richards, R. (2008). "Helping Children with Learning Disabilities Understand What They Read." *LD Online*. [Online Publication]. Retrieved from http://www.ldonline.org/article/Helping_Children_with_Learning_Disabilities_Understand_What_They_Read. Accessed July 16, 2009.

Scadden, L. (2008). *Surpassing Expectations: My Life without Sight.* Xlibris Corporation.

Schmetzke, A. (April 2001). "Online Distance Education: 'Anytime, Anywhere' But Not for Everyone." *Information Technology and Disability Journal*, 7(2). Retrieved from http://people.rit.edu/easi/itd/itdv07n2/axel.htm. Accessed June 27, 2009.

Shank, P. (2005). "The Value of Multimedia in Learning." Retrieved from http://www.adobe.com/designcenter/thinktank/valuemedia/. Accessed July 25, 2009.

Suzuki, M., & Yamaguchi, K., (2008). "Math-Document Accessibility with Infty-Reader and Chatty-Infty." Paper presented at the 23rdAnnual International Technology & Persons with Disabilities Conference, CSUN 2008, Los Angeles, CA, March 10–15, 2008.

U.S. Department of Education Office of Civil Rights Case Docket No. 09–95-2006. "Letter of January 25, 1996 addressed to Dr. Robert Caret, President, San Jose State University." Retrieved from http://uwctds.washington.edu/policy/09952206.RES.htm. Accessed July 25, 2009.

U.S. Department of Education Office of Civil Rights Case Docket No. 09–97-2002. Letter of April 7, 1997 addressed to Dr. James Rosser, President, California State University, Los Angeles. Retrieved from http://uwctds.washington.edu/policy/09972002.RES.htm. Accessed July 25, 2009.

U. S. Department of Education Office of Civil Rights Case Docket No. 09–97-6001. Letter of January 22, 1998 addressed to Thomas J. Nussbaum, Chancellor, California Community Colleges, Sacramento. Retrieved from http://icdri.org/legal/ocrsurltr.htm. Accessed March 13, 2010.

U. S. Department of Education Office of Civil Rights Case Docket No. 09–03-2166. Letter of September 1, 2003 addressed to Milton A. Gordon, President, California State University, Fullerton. Retrieved from www.tc3.edu/bcl/altformhandbook/OCR CSUFullerton case.DOC. Accessed July 25, 2009.

U. S. Department of Justice. (2005). *A Guide to Disability Rights Laws.* Civil Rights Division, Disability Rights Section. September 2005. [Online Publication]. Available at http://www.ada.gov/cguide.htm. Accessed July 13, 2009.

U. S. Government Accountability Office. (October 2009). GAO Report GAO 10–33. *Higher Education and Disability: Education Needs a Coordinated Approach to Improve Its Assistance to Schools in Supporting Students.* Retrieved from http://www.gao.gov/new .items/d1033.pdf. Accessed February 18, 2010.

W3C Web Accessibility Initiative (October 17, 2008). "Web Accessibility Quicktips: WCAG 2 at a Glance." [Online Publication]. Retrieved from http://www.w3c.org/ WAI/WCAG20/glance/. Accessed February 21, 2010.

RESOURCES

The value of connecting with resources on the Internet is that they can be kept up-to-date in a way not possible for print resources. These resources are only the tip of what is available.

ASSOCIATIONS

- AHEAD (American Association on Higher Education and Disabilities) is an association of college and university professional staff who work in support departments for students with disabilities.

  http://www.ahead.org

- ATHEN (Access Technologists Higher Education Network) is a professional organization for technologists working in the field of accessible technology in higher education.

  http://www.athenpro.org

BRAILLING SERVICES

Dozens of commercial and nonprofit Braille production companies are available to colleges wishing to outsource Braille production. The majority of these resources have Web addresses and accept electronic submission of materials to be Brailled. Prices, production times, and quality vary.

- The American Printing House for the Blind, Inc.

  http://www.aph.org/contact.htm

- Braille Jymico Inc.

  http://www.braillejymico.qc.ca/products.htm

- Braille Transcribers

  http://www.spedex.com/directories/braille.htm

- gh, LLC, specializes in technical Braille and tactile graphics

  http://www.gh7.com/braille.htm

CAPTIONING SERVICE PROVIDERS

- Automatic Sync Technologies, LLC—Web-based video captioning with quick turnaround

  http://web.automaticsync.com

- Caption Colorado—Both captions for existing media and real time captioning

  http://www.captioncolorado.com/

- eCaptions—General captioning with a specialty in education applications

  http://www.ecaptions.com/

- National Captioning Institute—Captioning for broadcast and Internet delivery

  http://www.ncicap.org/

- The National Center on Accessible Media (NCAM)—Besides captioning, NCAM has developed MAGpie software to help individuals do their own captioning

  http://www.wgbh.org/ncam

CONFERENCES

There are many conferences on disabilities with a component on technology aimed at various audiences. These conferences have a strong education component.

- Accessing Higher Ground, sponsored by the University of Colorado, focuses on postsecondary education and alternative media.

  http://www.colorado.edu/atconference/

- California State University Northridge—The Conference on Assistive Technology and Persons with Disabilities has provided an inclusive setting for researchers, practitioners, exhibitors, end users, speakers, and other participants to share knowledge and best practices in the field of assistive technology.

http://www.csun.edu/cod/conference

ELECTRONIC BOOKS ON THE INTERNET FOR PEOPLE WITH DISABILITIES

- Bookshare.org—An online digital repository of electronic books available exclusively for people with certified disabilities

http://www.bookshare.org

- National Library Service Library of Congress—The Library of Congress has provided books for people with certified visual disabilities for over seventy-five years and now are expanding into books in a digital format.

http://lcweb.loc.gov/nls/nls.html

- Recording for the Blind and Dyslexic—RFB&D provides books primarily for students. It has moved from audio disks to cassettes and now to digital books.

http://www.rfbd.org

GOVERNMENT RESOURCES

- U.S. Department of Education, National Institute on Disability and Rehabilitation Research—Research related to the rehabilitation of individuals with disabilities.

http://www2.ed.gov/about/offices/list/osers/nidrr/index.html

- U.S. Department of Education, Office of Special Education and Rehabilitative Services—Committed to improving results and outcomes for people with disabilities of all ages.

http://www2.ed.gov/about/offices/list/osers/index.html

- National Science Foundation—Department of Research in Disabilities Education seeks to broaden the participation and achievement of people with disabilities in all fields of science, technology, engineering, and mathematics.

http://www.nsf.gov/funding/pgm_summ.jsp?pims_id=5482

- U.S. Department of Justice. A Guide to Disability Rights Laws—Includes the Rehabilitation Act Sections 504 and 508 as well as the Americans with Disabilities Act.

  http://www.ada.gov/cguide.htm

INTERNET WEB SITES ON ACCESSIBLE INFORMATION TECHNOLOGY

- DAISY Consortium—Digital Accessible Information System is the organization promoting electronic document standards that make electronic books more navigable similar to print documents.

  http://www.daisy.org/

- DO-IT (Disabilities, Opportunities, Internetworking, and Technology)—The Web site contains resources about disabilities and accessible electronic information.

  http://www.washington.edu/doit/

- EASI (Equal Access to Software and Information)—EASI provides online courses and live Webinars on up-to-date accessible information technology.

  http://easi.cc

- GRADE (Georgia Tech Research on Accessible Distance Education)—Improving the accessibility of distance education by technical assistance, training, and research.

  http://www.catea.gatech.edu/grade

- LD OnLine is the leading Web site on learning disabilities, learning disorders, and differences: ADD / ADHD, dyslexia, dysgraphia, dyscalculia, dysnomia, reading difficulties, speech and related disorders.

  http://www.ldonline.org/

- LD OnLine: Technology—Assistive technology including devices, software, recordings, and much more can increase the capabilities of individuals with disabilities. Also, technology that is used by everyone, such as spell check, can be particularly helpful to people with learning disabilities.

  http://www.ldonline.org/indepth/technology

- University of Illinois: Web Accessibility Best Practices—Best practices focus on functional rather than technical requirements.

  http://cita.disability.uiuc.edu/html-best-practices/index.php

- Web Accessibility Initiative (WAI) is the part of the World Wide Web Consortium (W3C) that sets guidelines for accessibility for the Internet and for related applications.

  http://www.w3.org/WAI/

- WebAIM (Web Accessibility in Mind)—Contains rich information on accessible information technology and provides detailed tutorials on how to do that.

  http://www.webaim.org

VENDORS OF ASSISTIVE TECHNOLOGY

- Adobe Accessibility Resource Center—Support for creating accessible Flash and PDF.

  http://www.adobe.com/accessibility/index.html

- ai squared—Screen magnification software.

  http://www.aisquared.com

- Apple—Accessibility—Apple includes assistive technology in its products as standard features.

  http://www.apple.com/accessibility/

- Design Science—Creator of powerful math authoring and display tools including MathType and MathPlayer.

  http://www.dessci.com/en/

- Freedom Scientific—Software for visually impaired and learning disabled people.

  http://freedomscientific.com

- gh, LLC—Helps people with print disabilities access textbooks, publications, standardized tests, or Web sites.

  http://www.gh-accessibility.com/

- GW Micro—Software for the visually impaired.

  http://www.gwmicro.com/

- Kurzweil Educational Systems—Kurzweil 1000 provides blind users access to printed and electronic materials. Scanned print documents and digital files such as eBooks or e-mail are converted from text to speech and read aloud.

  Kurzweil 3000 is a reading, study skill, and writing program that educators can use to meet the needs of struggling learners, including ELL students and students with special needs.

  http://www.kurzweiledu.com/

- LecShare, Inc.—Converts PowerPoint to QuickTime movies, accessible HTML, video podcasts and Word handouts.

  http://lecshare.com/

- Microsoft accessibility support—Information about accessibility features in Microsoft applications and its operating systems.

  http://www.microsoft.com/ENABLE/

- Netcentric Technologies—The PDF Accessibility Wizard (PAW) is an add-in for Word that will produce fully accessible PDF documents and walk authors through any needed corrections.

  http://www.net-centric.com/

- Nuance—Dragon NaturallySpeaking Speech Recognition Software—Popular voice recognition program.

  http://www.nuance.com/naturallyspeaking/

- ViewPlus Technologies, Inc.—Ink and Braille printers, Braille translation software, and accessibility products.

  http://www.viewplus.com

- Virtual508.com—The Accessible Wizard creates documents that are more accessible and usable by everyone, including people with disabilities.

  http://virtual508.com/

INDEX

A

Accessibility: defined, x; importance of, xii–xiii

Accessibility checkers, online, 85–87, 88

Accessible online course content, 23–29

Accessible Wizard for Office products, 79, 84–85, 86

Achecker accessibility evaluation tool, 86–87, 88

ADA compliance office, 123

Adaptive technology: defined, ix, 1–2; most commonly used, 2–6; skill of the student in using, 19, 29–30

Administration support for online learning, 122–123

Adobe Acrobat Reader application, 76, 77, 81

Adobe Web site, 77

Alt text labels, 48, 50–51, 55, 65, 71, 96

American Foundation for the Blind (AFB) report, 19, 20–21, 23, 143–152

Americans with Disabilities Act (ADA), 11, 12, 13, 122, 123

Angel (Learning Management Systems product), 21

Animation, avoiding, 66, 71, 102

Assisted or adaptive technologies, defined, ix, 1–2

Assistive technologies most commonly used: captioning and audio transcriptions, 5–6; on-screen keyboard, 3, 60; screen magnification software, 3–4, 20, 21, 28, 46, 60, 96; screen readers, 4–5, 20, 21, 27–28, 36, 53, 60, 96; voice recognition technology, 2–3, 60. *See also* Captioning

Audience for this book, x–xi

Audio transcriptions and video captioning, 5–6, 26, 105. *See also* Captioning

Automatic timing in PowerPoint, 67, 71

Awareness and skills training, 120–122

B

Bailey, B., 102, 103

Blackboard: opening screen in, 22; students' experiences with, 20–21, 144, 145, 146, 148

Blind and visually impaired students: color blindness issues, 26–27, 46; narrated slide shows and, 67–68;

screen magnification software for, 3–4, 20, 21, 28, 46, 60, 96; screen readers for, 4–5, 20, 21, 27–28, 36, 53, 60, 96; survey of, 20–21, 143–152; tactile graphics for, 14, 51, 96–98; video descriptions for, 103, 110–112

Braille, embossed hard copy, 14, 79, 120

Braille embossers, 79, 97–98

C

Camtasia, captioning with, 104, 106, 107–112

Captioning: Camtasia for, 104, 106, 107–112; as commonly used assistive technology, 5–6; MAGpie for, 106–107; for multimedia presentations, 26; for narrated slide shows, 70; open versus closed, 110; Web Content Accessibility Guidelines and, 16

Center for Applied Special Technology (CAST), 8, 9

Checkers, online accessibility, 85–87, 88

Checklist to help implement Web Content Accessibility Guidelines, 129–142

Chunking, 24–25, 35

Clark, R., 25

Closed captioning, 110

Color: careful use of, 26–27; contrasting, 24; of text and background, 46, 63–64, 65

Color blindness, 26, 46

Conferencing, Web, 28–29, 112

Contrast between foreground and background, 63–64, 65

Course content: captions and, 26; careful use of color in, 26–27; chunks, 24–25, 35; features of accessible, 23–24; learner-centered, 24; tables and spreadsheets, 27–28; text equivalents for every nontext element in, 25–26; Web conferencing and, 28–29, 112

D

DAISY (Digital Accessible Information System) format, 79–80

Data tables: Excel spreadsheets, 51–52, 53–55, 80; headers for, 27–28; in Microsoft Word, 51–53; in PowerPoint presentations, 66

Delta Alpha Pi Honor Society, 121–122

Dennett, J., 21

Department of Education's Office for Civil Rights (OCR), decisions of, 11, 12–15, 18, 115

Descriptive video, 103, 110–112

Desire to Learn (Learning Management Systems product), 21

Dick, T., 90, 96

Digitized information, as breakthrough, 1, 17

Distributing accessible content: from Excel spreadsheets, 80; file types and, 73–74; online accessibility checkers and, 85–87, 88; from PowerPoint presentations, 80–85; take-aways from chapter on, 88; from Word documents, 74–80

Document navigation: chunking and, 25; DAISY format and, 79, 80; table of contents and, 47

Dyslexia and voice recognition technology, 2–3

Dysnumeria, 51, 89

E

Effective communication, 13, 15

Embedded hyperlinks, issues with, 67

Engagement, multiple means of, 10

Equation Editor, 93

Excel spreadsheets: creating, 51–52, 53–55; distributing, 80

F

Facebook, 104
File converter, free, 74
File types, 73–74
Financial support for online learning, 123
Flash, Adobe, 104
Flexibility in use, 7
Font or typeface, guidelines for choosing a, 46, 59, 71
Font size: in PowerPoint presentations, 64–65; in Word documents, 46
Friedman, T., 24

G

Gardner, J., 96
Graphics: in PowerPoint, 65; relevant, 25, 59; tactile, 14, 51, 96–98; technical, 95–98; in Word, 48, 50–51

H

Headers for tables, 27–28
Heading styles in Microsoft Word, 37
Headings or subheads, usefulness of, 35–36
Hearing impairment, students with: captioning for, 5–6, 103, 106–110, 111; chunking of lessons for, 24–25; narrated slide shows and, 61, 68, 70; transcripts for, 103, 105
HTML content, use of, 21, 78–79, 83, 86, 124
Hyperlinks and buttons in PowerPoint, 67

I

Images: hidden text descriptions for, 25; in PowerPoint, 65; in Word, 48, 50–51. *See also* Technical graphics

Institution-wide support for accessible online learning: administration support, 122–123; awareness and skills training, 120–122; student disability services, 119–120; support team, 115–119; take-aways from this book on, 123–125
International Web accessibility laws and standards, 15–17
International World Wide Web Consortium (W3C), 15

J

JAWS screen reader, 53
Jones, R., 92

K

Kaplan, D., 21
Keyboards, on-screen, 3, 60
Kubiak-Becker, E., 90, 96

L

Laws and standards, international Web accessibility, 15–17
Learner-centered approach to teaching and learning, 24
Learning management systems (LMS): issues common to, 21–23; as leg of online learning tripod, 19; as part of online learning infrastructure, 19–20; students' experiences with, 20–21
LecShare Pro, 70, 83–84
Legal responsibility of administration, 122–123
Legislation, U.S. federal: Americans with Disabilities Act, 11, 12, 13, 122, 123; Office for Civil Rights (OCR) and, 12–15, 18; Rehabilitation Act, 10, 11–12, 13, 17, 122, 123, 127–128

Support team for institution-wide support: members of, 116; policies and procedures for, 118–119; questions on forming, 115–116; three groups to support, 117–118

Suzuki, M., 99

T

Table of contents in Microsoft Word, creating a, 47–48, 49

Tables: headers for, 27–28; in PowerPoint presentations, 66; in Word documents, 51–53. *See also* Excel spreadsheets

Tactile graphics, 14, 51, 96–98

Talking books, digital, 79

Taylor slate, 90

Technical graphics: issues with, 95–96; tactile version of, 14, 51, 96–98

Templates, description of, 34, 38, 39, 40. *See also* Styles, Microsoft Word's

Text boxes in PowerPoint, 66, 71

Text chat, 23

Text equivalent for every nontext element, 25–26, 127

Text formats, 76

Textbooks in alternative formats, 120

Three components of online accessibility: course content, 19, 23–29; learning management system (LMS), 19–23; student skill, 19, 29–30; take-aways from chapter on, 30–31

Timeliness of delivery, 13–14, 15

Title II of Americans with Disabilities Act, 11, 12, 13, 122, 123

Tolerance for error, 7

Toolbar checkers, 87

Training workshops to provide online accessibility, 121

Transcripts: captions versus, 26; creating, 105; importance of, 5

Twitter, 104

Typeface, guidelines for choosing a, 46, 59, 71

U

"Undue burden" exemption, 12, 14–15

Universal design: defined, 2, 6; PowerPoint and, 57–59; seven principles of, 7–8

Universal Design for Learning (UDL) movement: description of, 8; three primary principles of, 9–10; Web Content Accessibility Guidelines (WCAG 2.0) and, 16–17

Up-to-date technology on student's end, 29

V

Video captioning, 5–6, 106–110

Video descriptions, 103, 110–112

ViewPlus Technologies, 98

Visually impaired students: color blindness issues, 26–27, 46; narrated slide shows and, 67–68; screen magnification software for, 3–4, 20, 21, 28, 46, 60, 96; screen readers for, 4–5, 20, 21, 27–28, 36, 53, 60, 96; survey of, 20–21, 143–152; tactile graphics for, 14, 51, 96–98; video descriptions for, 103, 110–112

Visuals, relevant, 25, 59. *See also* Graphics

Voice recognition technology, 2–3, 60

W

WAVE (Web accessibility evaluation tool), 86, 87

Web Accessibility Initiative (WAI), 15, 16

CPSIA information can be obtained at www.ICGtesting.com
Printed in the USA
BVOW02n0538120514

352954BV00010BC/18/P